What It's Like
to be Amish

What It's Like to be Amish

*Reflections of an Amish farmer,
grandfather, historian, and storyteller*

Sam S. Stoltzfus

WALNUT
STREET
BOOKS

LANCASTER,
PENNSYLVANIA

Design by Cliff Snyder

Front cover photo: Dervin Witmer/Shutterstock.com
Back cover top photo: Greg Kelton/Dreamstime.com
Back cover bottom photo: Jeffrey Hutchinson/Dreamstime.com

What It's Like to be Amish is published by
Walnut Street Books, Lancaster, Pennsylvania
info@walnutstreetbooks.com

International Standard Book Number: 9781947597020

Library of Congress Control Number: Data available

Table of Contents

Hello, Everyone —

I am Pud's Sam, and my wife is Katie. My dad, Gideon B. Stoltz-fus, was known as "Pud,"* and I'm often called "Pud's Sam" so that I'm not confused with all of the other Sam Stoltzfuses in our local Amish community.

We live in Lancaster County, Pennsylvania, close to the Pequea Creek, the village of Gordonville, and busy Amtrak lines. The Pequea runs through Lancaster County, flowing west from the Welsh Mountains in the east to the Susquehanna River, creating a shallow valley 35 miles long.

Katie and I have nine children, seven of whom are married. We live on a 40-acre dairy farm, in the *Doddyhaus*. Our son Gideon and his family live in the main farm house. I've operated a shed and gazebo business and help with the farming when I'm needed. We also process horseradish to sell.

My hobby is freelance writing, especially telling about events happening in our neighborhood, in our church, and in our family during the last 50 years or longer.

Welcome to my memories and stories. I hope they give you

---

* Worried that her tiny infant son was not gaining weight as quickly as he should, *Dat's* mother fed him smashed bananas. He soon grew healthy and husky—and attracted the nickname "Pud" (short for "Pudding"), which stayed with him for the rest of his life.

a small window into what it's like to be Amish, from way back until now. You'll hear a little Pennsylvania Dutch now and then, our first language. I'm hoping that hearing these experiences stirs your memories, too.

The Old Order Amish of Lancaster County, Pennsylvania, gather for worship every other Sunday in the homes of their members. Some 20 to 40 households make up a church district, and the services are hosted by those members on a rotating basis. The Amish speak Pennsylvania Dutch, a dialect. They use German Bibles and hymnbooks during their worship, which usually lasts about three hours, and is followed by a simple meal and visiting.

CHAPTER ONE

Going In With the Boys

Back in the summer of 1951, when I was eight years old and life seemed large and wondrous, a big event was coming up in my small boy's world: "Going in with the boys." In our Amish church services, this first happens usually when Amish boys turn nine.

We closely follow a routine for entering the house or barn where the church service will be held. At about 8:00 in the morning, the ministers walk in according to when they were ordained. They're typically followed by visitors (the men who are present but don't live in our district), and then come the married men, also by age, all walking in single file. The men usually sit on one side and the women on the other side.

Then the *haus doddy*, the man whose family is hosting church that day, comes outside at about 8:00 or so and tells the boys to get ready to go in to the house or barn. The boys always shake hands with the ministers and then sit on benches, usually behind the ministers. In our district in 1951 there were approximately 45 boys, so it took three to five minutes for all of the boys to enter, shake hands, and be seated. The service begins when someone announces the first hymn.

Going in with the boys is a big ritual in our Amish world. It is the first rite of passage between boyhood and being nearly an adult. The next big step is turning 16 and getting our own horse and buggy. Somewhat similar to the first day of school as a first-grader, going in with the boys is a big milestone.

In 1951, my cousin Johnny had been going in with the big boys for over a year already. His brother Chester was a bit younger than me, and we both hoped that our time would soon come. We were double cousins—our fathers were brothers, and our mothers were sisters—so our genes were maybe about the same. Every Sunday morning, we'd watch with near envy as the boys were going in, looking so big and important.

My mother's stipulation

But there was one big task I had to do first. My mother insisted that I had to memorize the "Lobelied" (Hymn of Praise), the 28-line hymn which is always the second hymn sung at Amish church services. This felt like a big task for an eight-year-old with lots of other things to read. I had learned several small prayers and the Lord's Prayer before this, but the "Lobelied" was harder. There were four verses with seven lines each, all in High German. I recall saying it again and again, a verse at a time, often stumbling over a word or two. *Mam* would praise me, but frown if I missed a word.

All through August I worked hard, but try as I might, I didn't quite know every line by my ninth birthday on September 8th, so *Mam* said I would not go in with the boys. That following Sunday when we had church, I felt rather disturbed. All the church boys knew when my birthday was, and they all wondered why I didn't go in with them. Most likely, as any small boy would, I thought *Mam* would allow me to go in with the boys even if I didn't quite know the "Lobelied," but she didn't permit any shortcuts. One of my church buddies, Samuel Beiler, turned nine on September 23rd, and he was allowed to go in with the boys, even if he didn't know the "Lobelied."

So it was study more and recite more and more "*O Gott Vater wir loben Dich*" and all that followed, until finally I could say the 28 lines without missing a syllable. *Mam* smiled and said, "Now you may go in with the boys."

Also at age nine, boys got low shoes and a telescoped hat. I recall how special I felt with my new shiny shoes and my new hat as I got ready to go in with the boys.

Watching the big boys

I don't recall where church was that day, but I remember that I walked there, first going out the back field lane to my cousin's farm, carrying my shoes so they wouldn't get dusty. At my cousin's place, I put on my shiny, black patent leather shoes, and then we walked across their meadow and over the Pequea Creek on a creaky foot bridge. We were a foursome—10-year-old Johnny, eight-year-old Chester, seven-year-old Sam I., and me. We walked up Paradise Lane to the farm where church was being held and stood by the barn hill, watching the big boys—those over 16—drive in with their horses and buggies. We always knew who had the fastest horse and which harness was the fanciest.

Finally at 8:00 or so, the farm's owner came and said, "Get ready to go in."

The big boys would comb their hair, one holding the mirror while another combed. A comb and mirror were prized possessions. We'd all use the "rest room" (a nearby horse stall or corner in the barn) and then we were ready. Soon after 8:00, the farmer would come and lead us in.

Mam made sure I understood that I should shake hands just

with the ministers, the ones with their hats on, and not all of the older men. The men who were not ordained would remove their hats when the boys came in; the ministers took their hats off when all the boy were seated and the hymn was announced. We boys put our hats on the empty benches or in a nearby shed.

I well recall how good it felt to walk in with the boys that first time. I remember shaking hands with the ministers. They looked so reverent with their hats on—Amos U. with his old, wise face; Ephraim, who always had a smile; Uncle Sylvan looking so kind; Deacon Aaron who was last and had such twinkling eyes. Finally, we boys were all seated on the pine benches. I was the next to last one. Someone announced the first hymn, and the service started.

There we sat, Sammy Beiler and me, holding the *Ausbund* hymnbook. When the "Lobelied" was started, I helped along with the lines. All forenoon we had to sit still and listen to the preacher. Most likely the text was John 3. *Mam* had warned me that if I didn't behave, I'd have to sit with her. I recall it happened once or so!

Amish boys go in with the boys till they move into their own homes. Weddings are usually held in late fall, and then in the spring, the newlyweds move into their own homes and start housekeeping. From then on, the husband goes in with the men and the wife with the women. This is the next rite of passage. Going in with the boys is over.

CHAPTER TWO

The First and Last Amish Parachute Jump

It was one of the first nice days of spring back in 1954 when three of my cousins—Johnny, Chester, and Sam—and I were out on a Sunday afternoon trek. You could call it a small boy safari. For us young boys, imagination was 95% of our play. We were pirates on the high seas, cowboys running on the range, or Lewis and Clark on their expedition.

We started out our field lane, wandered across the fields and along the fence rows. We decided to check out Pete Lapp's trash hole, or to state it properly, the neighborhood dump. Years ago it had been a small quarry, and then later a place for neighbors to dump their trash. Remember, this was in 1954. There were no garbage trucks or dumpster boxes. Folks just threw their rubbish in such places. We found broken toys, hay strings, baler wire, and worn-out farm implements.

Hey, what's this? Looks like a big sheet of plastic about 20 feet square. "Look what I found!" I called to my cousins. "Let's make a parachute."

I don't recall my cousins' reactions, but there were some words. Johnny said, "Huh. . . you'll be too scared to use it."

Chester said, "I'm not jumping off anything more than six feet off the ground with that parachute."

Sam said, "Yes, I'll help make it, but you must take the first jump."

So we all yanked the plastic out of the trash pile, cleaned it up, and lugged it back to our barn 500 yards away. Now you must remember those ancient times way back in the mid-1900s. A big sheet of plastic was as scarce as a straight-A report card.

These three boys were my double first cousins. Our dads were brothers, and our moms were sisters, so our genes were similar. But my uncle's boys always seemed a bit ahead of me in common sense. Our farms were three-quarters of a mile apart. Our dads shared hay and threshing equipment, sold their crops together, and were in the same church district, so we were often together making hay, cutting corn, and threshing. So it's no small wonder that they loved the parachute idea but didn't want to be the jumper.

The plan

We took a big pile of strings and knotted them together to make parachute strings and a sort of harness to go around my belt and under my seat to fasten the parachute to the jumper. We talked about braiding the strings, but our impatience to make the first jump soon squashed that idea. It didn't take us long to make the parachute, even if we had no directions. By now the cousins were clapping their hands with glee. They could hardly wait to see me take the first jump. Me. . . I was getting a bit sweaty and wished I had never thought of such a dumb thing as an Amish Parachute Jumper.

We decided the first practice jump would be in the barn from the timbers to the four-foot-deep straw mow. We tied the parachute to my body. Johnny crawled up first, carrying the parachute. He stood on the tobacco rails four feet above me and held the chute. Chester and Sam were to the left and right of Johnny, keeping the chute spread out. I stood there a bit, then jumped, plop, into the loose straw! I wasn't sure if the chute slowed my fall or not. The cousins weren't sure either, so Practice Jump Number 2 was necessary.

Wise Johnny seemed to think I must go way up to the peak of the barn for the next jump, so back up the ladder and up to the top tobacco rail I went. Johnny and Chester stood on either side, holding up the chute. Cousin Sam was on the rails yelling, "Come on! Jump, Sammy!"

More daring

Wow, it looked so-o-o far down to the straw mow. (It was only 25 feet or so.) I jumped, and sure enough, I felt some tugs from the baler twine harness. Now I was ready to jump again and prove that the chute worked, or so I thought.

The brave jumper and his parachute bearers marched outside and crossed the barnyard to the chicken house where Jump Number 3 would take place. Up the ladder we went and onto the roof. It was a breezy spring day, and the air readily filled the parachute, so that I had to pull on the strings to get to the high part of the roof. This time I didn't hesitate because I knew the parachute worked. . . or so I thought. I ran across the roof, my chute-bearers faithfully running with me, and then I jumped up as high as I could, and into space I went.

KERPLOP! I hit the ground like a rock. If the chute slowed me down, it sure wasn't noticeable. I had terrible pain in my back, side, and bottom. And my pride was hurt to the nth degree. I recall hollering and moaning while the cousins were bent double with laughter. No pity for poor me!

Well, they cut the parachute harness loose, and we put the chute back on the trash pile. That was the last Amish Parachute Jump.

I recall limping to the house and lying on the couch, trying to nurse my pride back to normal. At first my cousins thought I was hurt, although I don't think they had a cupful of sympathy. Once they saw I wasn't hurt much, Johnny, Chester, and Sam went home (it was chore time), still laughing, clearly not realizing the significant part of history they had witnessed.

The Pennsylvania Dutch word for Dad is **Dat,** *for Mother or Mom is* **Mam,** *for Grandfather or Grandpa is* **Doddy,** *for Grandmother or Grandma is* **Mommy.** *For Great-Grandfather, the word is* **Grosdoddy,** *and for Great-Grandmother, the word is* **Grosmommy.**

CHAPTER THREE

When *Doddy* Closed in His Buggy

In 1960, when I was 17, *Doddy* Sam said, "Sammy, let's close in our carriage so we won't freeze our noses going to church when it's cold!" Of course I was glad to help.

So one day *Doddy* and I took the shafts off their carriage and pushed it into the shop, fired up the stove, and the fun began. *Doddy* had suffered a stroke in 1954, which made his left hand weak. He couldn't use power tools, but he could tell me how to do the work. I enjoyed working with him, and *Doddy* was a good teacher.

Doddy was born in 1882, got married in 1908, and then worked four years in Eli Riehl's carriage shop near Lancaster, where he became an accomplished carriage-maker. After he quit farming in 1945, he built carriage and buggy bodies for Harry Moore, who had a buggy shop in Ronks. I can recall many days in my childhood when I watched *Doddy* in his shop making a carriage body, assembling it all with hand tools.

Now *Doddy* took out the front seat and cut off each end so there would be space for a sliding door to roll past. *Mommy* redid the cushion fabric at each end.

Next *Doddy* showed me how to make door sills and seat rails. We got a stack of oak and poplar boards out of the shop upstairs and put them through the planer. We made the oak boards ¾" thick and the poplar ½" thick. Then I cut the poplar boards and fitted them into the front of the carriage to make the dashboard. Next we made an oak sill for the windows to slam against.

Doddy heated up his stinky, animal-hide glue. He showed me how to first fit and screw the boards on dry, then take them off, spread the glue on them, quickly clamp the boards on, and run in the screws before the glue set.

Doddy the tutor

Doddy was very patient with his greenhorn helper. In his prime working days, he could have done the job in a day or so. But for this project, we just worked at it in my spare time, because my main job was helping *Dat* do the farm chores. In fact, helping *Doddy* gave me a great excuse to slip out of the barn work. For me, shop work was much more fun than barn chores.

The next part of the project was making the doors and windows. *Doddy* showed me how to rip poplar boards and cut out the window frames on his gas, engine-powered table saw. We put the frames together, cut glass from some old window sash, and fit the glass in as we assembled the windows and doors.

Our next job was painting. *Doddy* instructed me to give all the bare wood a coat of gray primer, then sand the boards, and finish them with a coat of glossy black. *Doddy* did some of the painting, showing me how to brush with vertical strokes so the paint wouldn't run. I recall that we painted the whole carriage because it hadn't been painted for years. *Mommy* looked pleased to see such a shiny carriage, although she expressed some fears that the church people would wonder why these old folks had to have such a shiny, black, closed carriage.

Doddy said, "Humph! You're the one who always wants to stay home if it's cold. Now we can go to church in comfort."

Our last step was putting in the doors and windows and making a bonnet to fit over the front windows, so, as *Doddy* said, "It would look like a market wagon."

How buggies have changed

Let me explain a little about Lancaster Amish carriage history. Soon after the Civil War, many plain folks started going into the city of Lancaster to operate farmers market stands. They always traveled by open buggies, and due to dusty roads and sometimes driving rain or snow, the market goods didn't always arrive in good condition. So the church leaders permitted these wagons to be closed in. They came to be known as "market wagons." They were eight to nine feet long and quite heavy, and they were drawn by two horses.

On Sundays, we were not to hitch up our teams (the Ten Commandments teach us not to work on Sundays), so folks walked to church. Only elderly women or boys rode horseback. By 1880 or so, open carriages were permitted on Sundays, as well as open buggies for courting-age youth. And either by default or convenience, market wagons were getting shorter and lighter, and big families and the elderly began using them to go to church services. This became more common between 1930 and 1940.

Then around 1950 or so, some daring Lower Pequea or Conestoga carriage-maker installed sliding doors, windows, and a canvas dashboard in open carriages, and closed them in. Of course, our more conservative Upper and Middle Pequea church leaders, as well as those in the Millcreek district, frowned on this.

Progress and comfort prevailed, and the storm front, as it was called, was here to stay. Soon the canvas dash was replaced by a permanent wooden dash, and light switches were mounted on the dash. Even a glove box was added. But the more conservative folks always wanted a bonnet to keep the traditional market wagon look. However, a carriage had its rear wheels *behind* the carriage. A market wagon had its rear wheels *under* the body by about eight inches. Today, carriage and market wagon bodies are the same size, 38″ wide and 72″ long, but their running gears are different.

Doddy showed me how to fire up the forge and bend ½″ rods to make the bonnet frame. Then we stitched canvas over it—and the old carriage now looked like a market wagon.

Rehabbing a still-working antique

Doddy was married in 1908, and in those first years, he and *Mommy* used an open buggy. *Doddy* had made this carriage that he and I were working on in 1915, when he and *Mommy* first had children, so it was nearly 50 years old. *Doddy* didn't have brakes on his carriage because he said it wasn't that heavy. *Doddy* wasn't much for a lot of modern fixtures. His carriage had never had battery lights either. But after the carriage was painted and the doors and windows were installed, he made a trip to Lancaster to buy two headlights, two taillights, wire, and switches. I did all the wiring.

It was a great milestone the day we pushed the carriage out of the shop and put the shafts back on, hitched up Silver the horse, and drove off to church. Outside it was freezing cold, but inside the carriage, *Doddy, Mommy,* and Aunt Liz were cozy and warm. *Mommy* was muttering, "Looks sort of fancy for old folks." (They were the only old folks in our district to have a closed carriage.) But *Doddy* was in his glory! He didn't need his heavy overcoat and thick gloves. He sat there in arm-chair comfort!

Mommy still heated bags of dried corn and put them in the carriage at our feet. That did feel cozy on cold days.

Doddy and *Mommy* used the rebuilt carriage for almost 12 more years until they died in 1971. At times when it was rainy or cold, I'd ask *Doddy* if I could use the carriage to go see my girlfriend, or if we had a double date I'd use it sometimes. I recall once when it was rainy over Easter and I had made a bookcase for my girlfriend, I used the closed carriage to deliver the furniture. It arrived in fine shape.

Now today, more than 45 years later, I am still grateful for those skills *Doddy* taught me when we closed in the carriage.

CHAPTER FOUR

A Railroad Move to Kansas

My great-grandparents moved to Kansas in 1885. Joel Fisher was born in 1842 near Ronks in eastern Lancaster County. Elizabeth Fisher was born in 1844 in Groffdale, a few miles north of Ronks. They married in 1867 and first lived along Bachmantown Road, south of Ronks. Some eight years later they moved onto the Blue Gate Farm on Route 30, just west of Ronks Road.

In 1863, President Abraham Lincoln signed the Pacific Railway Act, which gave the western railroads large tracts of land to build rail lines to the West Coast. After the Transcontinental Railroad was completed in 1869, real estate companies sold off lots from these lands which were not needed by the railroads. That explains why land agents came through the East, advertising cheap land that would grow lots of wheat, pasture cattle, and support whole new communities.

Joel Fisher caught the Kansas fever and bought a 640-acre tract and a 160-acre tract, without seeing the land. The family made plans to move west. After a two-day farm equipment sale, Joel and Elizabeth packed their possessions and headed for Harvey County, Kansas.

In late February of 1885, there was some unusual activity in the small village of Steam-Mill Crossing, today called Ronks. Along the Pennsylvania Railroad's main line, two boxcars packed with farm machinery and household goods, plus a passenger car, stood on the siding, coupled to a steam engine. A horse-drawn wagon pulled up to the station, which was merely a small roofed platform. Stepping off the wagon and boarding the train were Joel Fisher, 43; his wife Elizabeth, 36; and their children Daniel, 17; Nancy, 15; Lovina, 13; Lydia, 11; Stephen, 10; Emma, 8; Joe, 5; Joel, 3; and Salome (my grandmother), 10 months. Also boarding the train was the Amos Stoltzfus family: Amos, age 38; his wife Emma, 32; and their children Benuel, 12; Mary, 10; Kathryn, 8; Rachel, 5; and Sarah, 3.

Complicated traveling

The Fishers also took along their hired man, Pete Keener. It appears that 19 persons filled the passenger coach.

No doubt, as the train pulled out on that cold February morning, the cars were also filled with mixed feelings. The men and children were probably excited and glad to be traveling. The women may have been blinking back tears, wondering if they would ever see their homeland again.

Joel's and Elizabeth's baby Salome was my grandmother.

There are no records of this move, but by studying railroad maps and schedules, I've calculated how they might have traveled and how long it took. Railroads were barely in their second generation in 1885. There were open vestibule wood coaches, some air brakes, and no automatic couplers. Locomotives were hand-fired, small, 75- to 100-ton affairs. They had no super heaters, no automatic signals, no roller bearings. Most trains stopped every 50 miles for coal and every 100 miles for water. One hundred miles was considered a day's run.

The Fisher and Stoltzfus families traveled on what was known as an Emigrant Train, a service the Pennsylvania Railroad provided for families moving any great distance. A coach, several box cars, and a livestock car were coupled together, loaded with the families' goods. The rate was very reasonable.

With some imagination, one can contemplate the move west. The men and older boys probably kept busy visiting with the train crew as they took in the passing scenery. The women tried hard to be brave, blinking back tears as they left their homeland and extended families, not knowing when and if they would ever see them again.

According to 1885 railroad schedules, the train averaged 30 to 40 miles an hour. That means it took about 15 to 16 hours to get to Pittsburgh, arriving around midnight. Sleeping in the trains' seats probably wasn't the best place to spend the night. By late on the second day, they had likely reached Chicago.

Two other interesting facts:

- By railroad law, livestock had to be fed and watered every 10 hours.
- Back then, passenger trains stopped for meals that usually cost 25 cents each.

Changing trains in Chicago

In those days, the Pennsy terminated at Chicago, so all goods, livestock, and passengers had to transfer to another railroad. My dad recollects his uncle Steve saying that Dan drove the cattle through the streets of Chicago for about four miles, from the Pennsylvania Railroad's Englewood station to the LaSalle Street station where the western railroad trains began their runs.

Just picture the bedlam, with Dan driving the livestock, the men loading the goods onto wagons, and then at the other station, putting it all back onto railroad cars, the mothers busy caring for the little ones and hoping the older children didn't wander off. This transfer probably took a half-day or more.

Most likely the group left Chicago on the Atchison Topeka and Santa Fe Railway, whose lines ran west through Kansas City and Topeka, Kansas. The trip from Chicago through Illinois, Missouri, and into Kansas, stopping either in McPherson or Newton, probably took another 24 hours. It was now 3½ days since they had left Ronks. At that point they would have been about eight miles south of their new farms.

Railroads operated much differently then. Some engineers

always had the same locomotives with their names printed on the cab side, taking great pride in keeping them in good operating condition. Some almost lived in the cabs. Most likely the Amish men and older boys spent time each day in the cab, visiting and helping the train crew. It's said that one particularly friendly engineer took a liking to five-year-old Joe, letting him sit on his lap, operate some of the controls, and blow the whistle.

Later, Joe left home at age 20 and started working on the Pennsy, where he was employed for 40-some years (see pages 44-51). He and his brother Steve boarded with a Mennonite family in Philadelphia when they began working on the railroad. Joe first worked with the track gang, then moved to firing locomotives, and was promoted to engineer in about 1915. In his prime years, Joe, the Flying Dutchman, ran fast passenger trains from Harrisburg to New York and later ran commuter trains from Paoli to Philly.

So as the sun rose one morning in late February of 1885, the two families hauled their goods to their homes, which they were seeing for the first time. Joel built a new barn on his 160-acre farm. Amos Stoltzfus and his family lived on the same farm but in another homestead.

Hauling the goods that last eight to 10 miles to their new homes must have been quite a task. The two women tried to create some order and keep track of the children, who hadn't had proper rest for three or four days.

A hard landing

Joel and Elizabeth and their family stayed only two years. Because of the heat, drought, and dust storms, they weren't able to harvest any crops. Wheat was the main crop and the only cash crop. They returned to Lancaster County, Pennsylvania, in 1887. Amos and Emma Stoltzfus and their children stayed another year. They had to have church assistance to pay their train fare back to Lancaster.

My grandmother, Salome, born March 11, 1884, had faint memories of their Kansas home. She would have been almost three when they moved back. I grew up on the Sam and Salome Stoltzfus farm. They lived in our *Doddyhaus,* so *Mommy* told me some of these stories.

Her parents, Joel and Elizabeth Fisher, never talked about their Kansas move, probably because it wasn't a success. It must have seemed brave and adventuresome to travel 1500 miles to open country. The parents were likely hoping to have farms for all their children, like many families who start new communities today. But what a sad trip back to Ronks in 1887. Likely the children and their mothers were happy to be back in their homeland with the relatives.

The move seemed to give the boys travel fever. Joel, Jr. went to Oregon and settled there; Stephen set off for Kansas and John for Ohio. The boys all drifted to other faiths. All of the girls but Emma remained Amish.

Joel never regained his financial status. He had to sell his Route 30 farm soon after they moved back. Then he bought a farm in Limeville, near Gap, but had to sell it soon thereafter. The family lived on rented farms after that.

In their last years, Joel and Elizabeth lived with their children. Joel died in 1926; Elizabeth in 1942. They are both buried in the Ronks, Pennsylvania, cemetery.

Rather than dwelling on what may have been an unwise move to Kansas, let's think of the many new friends and contacts the Fisher and Stoltzfus families probably made.

CHAPTER FIVE

Home on the Range in Lancaster, Where One Buffalo Still Roams

Buffalo on the loose in eastern Lancaster County? Yes, siree, 12 750-pound bison bulls. They roamed over Salisbury Township and beyond, and on into the Welsh Mountain foothills, some for over eight weeks. One is still at large. *Vas is los?* (What's going on?)

There was a Stoltzfus of Leacock Township, an Amish cattleman and entrepreneur, and he decided to try a new venture: fatten buffalo bulls. Since the fat cattle market is as low as a sick steer's nose, he decided to try his hand at producing buffalo steak. There was another reason: he had just purchased a good farm in the White Horse hinterlands.

He thought, we can run buffalo in the large meadow. The Pequea Creek flows through it, which will make cheap buffalo grazing. So with lots of Lancaster County sunshine and plenty of Pequea Creek water, said bison will soon be as docile as fat steers. *Das war letz.* (That was wrong.)

The cattleman purchased his 12 buffalo, and they arrived at their new address in late April. The animals just loved it, romping in the meadow, drinking from the creek, behaving like fenced-in bovines should.

Then, on that historic day, May 3, one of the buffalo found an escape route where the fence crossed the creek. Quickly, using buffalo lingo, he informed the rest of the clan, and they were off, tails in the air, snorting through the vast Pequea plains. *Dot geh'n sie.* (There they go.) Maybe they were hoping to get to their ancestors' birthplace 1,500 miles west.

And romp and roam they did, through Salisbury and West Cain, stampeding through young corn and lush alfalfa, ripping through fences as if through spider webs. They tore across tobacco patches, got into gardens, and splattered up front lawns. *S'Macht die frau base.* (Makes the wife mad.) And they got into pastures with Holstein heifers for buffalo blind dates.

Who can do the job?

There are no instructions in the township code book about how to catch buffalo. Not yet. But the word was out: If you see a shaggy buffalo, call Stoltzfus pronto. Provided he hears his phone ring, he'll call Sam Kinsinger, who will grab his trusty dart carbine, call his pickup-truck driver, Al Workman, and head off to Pequea Valley.

Not since Henry Lapp's 180-horsepower tractor ran off and

dashed two miles cross-country—finally plowing into Ike Die-
ner's barn—was there such excitement in the *unner beckway*
(Lower Pequea), as we Amish call it. Sam and Al would drive to
the buffalo area, carefully stalk the target buffalo from downwind
to within 50 yards, take careful aim, and zing, wait until the tran-
quilizer took effect. The beast would turn turtle, the crew would
truss him up, and four or five hefty men would throw the sleeping bison on the pickup bed and dash back to the meadow he had
escaped. Quick—untie him before he comes to and *mea braucha
noch eins* (we have to catch another one).

Farmers plant their crops, spray for weeds, cultivate, and watch
things grow, and they take a dim view of any man or beast that
treads in their planted fields. So these buffalo ripping through
the fields were mighty unpopular. Henry Lapp (of escaped tractor fame) said, "If I see one, I'll shoot it with my 30/30 and it will
roam no more."

In the old days, there were two Amish cowboys who had
trained cow ponies and could rope them like Western cattlemen.
Leroy Esh and his trusty steed Queen, along with his hired man,
Elam Zook and his mount Maple, could rope heifers at a dead
gallop. Once, down in Nine Points, a farmer's 15 heifers went
wild, roaming Bart and Colerain townships for two days. Leroy
and Elam roped them all. Some Lancaster Stockyard professional
horsemen who were called out gave up the first day. But today,
Leroy and Elam, both gray-haired and their horses gone, don't
take to roping any more.

Mixed success

Stoltzfus and his buffalo-catching hands, Sam Kinsinger and Al Workman, did the best they could for weeks. Meanwhile, the buffalo crashed through the hinterlands, growing wilder and more feisty. One was shot three times, but into the woods he'd go and no one could find him. The beast got away again. *Kannsht mich net fanga!* (You can't catch me!)

Not since Revolutionary War soldiers roamed the Compass area, and were fed in the Welsh Mountain foothills during Washington's Valley Forge campaign, was there such a commotion in the *unner beckway* (Lower Pequea).

For 10 weeks, Stoltzfus and his crew chased these critters, catching them one by one. One was caught the first day, two the next day (on a Sunday), and finally all but one, which, as mentioned, is still considered to be at large.

So the word is out: Watch for the buffalo. Perhaps he is still indeed at large, or perhaps he's gift-wrapped and stacked in someone's freezer. The mystery of the lost Pequea buffalo continues. *Wu is er?* (Where is he?)

Note: This happened back in the 1900s.

CHAPTER SIX

The Differential

More than 175 years ago, the first practical, portable steam engine was made. It was a self-contained unit with the engine mounted on the boiler. These were later made by several manufacturers: Frick, J.J. Case, Peerless, and Avery. Mounted on four wheels, these engines powered threshing machines, sawmills, feed grinders, pumps, and shop machinery.

They were fitted with two or four horse hitches and pulled about with horses. Even later, when self-propelled engines became practical, some states had laws calling for a team of horses to be in front of these engines when they were traveling on a public road.

Slowly, steam engine companies made bigger and more powerful models. In 1885, J.J. Case offered a 16 horsepower engine that weighed 4½ tons. This was quite a load for horses.

During some of these early years, models were offered with one-wheel drive. Efforts were made to drive both wheels, but then turning was impossible. And at times the solid axle broke.

Then along came Eli Yost, an Amish farmer in Leacock Township, who lived some two miles northeast of Intercourse,

Pennsylvania. In about 1880, he developed the first practical differential. Apparently he had some shop tools and mechanical knowledge. He then asked his neighbor Jake Moore to help; Jake operated a blacksmith shop along Centerville Road. Jake either wasn't interested in this apparatus or didn't have the proper equipment to work with Eli. So Eli traveled the nine miles to Lancaster, knocked on the door of the Best Steam Engine Company, and explained what he wanted to have made. They also turned him down. They didn't think it would work or that there would be much demand.

Next, Eli traveled almost 100 miles to Waynesboro, Pennsylvania, to ask the Frick Company to take a look at his idea. Here was a big engine company making engines in six sizes. Again the answer was no. Eli was a determined individual. He was sure his idea must work. He said he didn't want any royalties; he just wanted a differential made for his own steam engine.

In this same neighborhood was the Geyser Peerless Engine Company, also a big, well-known manufacturer. Eli showed them his idea. No, they didn't think it would work.

Persistent and convinced

Probably quite disappointed, Eli returned home, still not able to have interested anyone in his idea. The following morning he traveled to Lancaster with plans to go on to Philadelphia, hoping to find someone who would make his invention. At the train station, he met Mr. Landis of the Best Machine Company, of Lancaster. Eli had earlier asked the company to make his differential but was turned down.

Mr. Landis asked, "Where are you going?"

Eli replied, "Going to Philly and hoping to find a shop that will make my invention."

"No need for that. I'll make your differential," Mr. Landis said. So the two men made an agreement. Mr. Landis formed the Eclipse Machine Company and made the first practical differential, patented it, and put one on Eli Yost's steamer. The rest is history.

Soon the Frick Company called on the Eclipse Machine Company. They came to an agreement and started to put the differential on their engines. Eventually the organization became the Frick Eclipse Company. It wasn't long before all steam engine and tractor manufacturers put this appliance on their products. When the automobile manufacturers started in the early 1900s, they also bought the manufacturing rights.

So today, thanks to the belief and persistence of one Amish farmer, we have this simple, three-bevel gear differential that lets one wheel go faster than the other on corners, but on straight roads, both pull equally.

Until 1960, differentials were made as Landis first designed them. Then Ford made a differential with a clutch system called "positraction," so that if one wheel was spinning in mud, the clutch would engage, making both wheels pull. This was particularly an advantage in trucks, heavy tractors, and construction equipment.

CHAPTER SEVEN

The Summer of the Bridge

Ever since God created our planet earth and divided the waters on the third day of creation, the Pequea Creek has flowed through our Lancaster County. Creeks and rivers provide water and drain the land, but they also create separations of land.

So it was with our Pequea Creek, which flows through my uncle's farm. Let me tell you how my cousins and I built a bridge over the soft, wide Pequea Creek in the summer of 1977.

It seemed that it shouldn't be all that complicated. We'd pour two concrete piers on each side, lay some beams across, place the roadway, and we'd have a bridge. Uncle Sylvan had made a bridge for Sammie Fisher in 1975, just a mile upstream, so we had a good example to follow.

After several rounds of talks, a serious meeting, and our careful inspection of Sammie's bridge, we began work in early June of 1977. Since cousin Sam was the farmer on whose land the bridge was being built, he was considered the manager. Cousin Chester did the design and blueprint work. The rest of Uncle's five boys and I helped.

First, we needed to contact the township about a permit, then go to the Pennsylvania Fish and Creek Association to get approval of our plans. An old-timer with a practical sense came out to the site and gave us the go-ahead, saying how high off the water and how big the piers needed to be, and so on. He gave us lots of good advice, all for the cost of the $50 permit. We were beginning to realize it was a big project, but things started to fall in place in many ways.

Finding materials

Thanks to another cousin, Dan Petersheim, we located a place that sold used steel. They had three 9' × 27' steel beams, each 50-some feet long, for a scrap price. We believed that the Lord was already answering prayers.

One evening we cousins went to inspect the beams and decided they would serve our purpose. Then on a Saturday we headed out early on the 50-mile trip to Hoover's Steel in Schwenksville (Montgomery County) to get the beams ready.

Cousin Sam threw us a curve at the steelyard. "Let's angle the bridge, so the farm lane won't have to make such a hard turn to cross the creek." After some practical discussions, cousin Chester drew the bridge outline on the steelyard parking lot with chalk lines. We all decided to put the south pier 15 feet downstream. Chester did some more drawing and decided the bridge would be placed at a 15 degree angle.

The 50-foot beams were marked off for cross beams and holes were drilled. The 6′ × 6′ steel crossbeams were cut and plates made. It was a bit late till we got home, tired but happy, yet we had the satisfaction of having gotten started.

The reason for the bridge

But I'm getting a bit ahead of my story. Back in June of 1976, Bishop Uncle Sylvan and his co-minister Ephraim King were killed on Route 30. Uncle's 300-foot farm lane ran straight onto heavily traveled Route 30. There was no other way out of the farm. Thus, the reason for this bridge. A south farm lane would be cut through the meadow, cross over the new bridge, and connect to Paradise Lane. Then the family wouldn't have to exit the farm lane onto busy Route 30.

It was kind of a healing process to work on the bridge. It was only a year before that Uncle left us so suddenly; cousin Chester had been ordained minister in his father's place. So as we worked together that summer, the focus was on the bridge and not on life's changes. All of us had full-time jobs. This bridge was a part-time project.

Early in June, Mike Fisher came and dug out the pier footers. We worked in knee-deep water making forms, and then tried to pump out the water just before we poured the concrete. Now we could work in the dry four inches above the water line, unless there was a heavy rain.

Next, we spent several weeks making forms and placing ¾"
R-bars. They were nothing fancy; plywood and 2 × 4s wired
together. The Fish and Creek man instructed us to first make
hooks in the R-bars for the wing walls and the pier walls, then
thread an R-bar through the hooks' upright to hook the walls
together in case the concrete cracked.

We worked on the project evenings and Saturdays. We planned
work days, and folks came to help. Finally, we were ready to pour
one side pier and the wing walls. It rained the day before, and
since we hadn't made the roadway first, as would have been
proper, the concrete trucks couldn't get to the job site, and pouring concrete was delayed.

Finally the meadow dried off, and the concrete was poured.
We removed the forms, floated them across the creek, and reset
them. We placed more rods. Cousin Sam manned the torch making the hooks on the R-bars. We got so skilled at form work and
rebar placing, that sometimes we even congratulated ourselves!

A side project?

Cousin Sam had Mike Fisher's crew make the 400-foot drive-
ways to the bridge site. Many loads of stone were spread and
graded. Then the concrete trucks could get to both ends of the
bridge site. We all had a busy (and, at times, hectic) schedule that
summer. We cousins were all full-time farmers. We each had cows

to milk, hay to make, and corn to cultivate. I also worked full-time for a Lancaster home builder, so I helped with the bridge mostly on evenings and Saturdays. Now and then I took some time off, but things didn't always go silky smooth.

We were double cousins. Our dads and mothers were brothers and sisters, so we almost thought and differed alike, including even arguing at times.

At the beginning of August, we scheduled a crane to come, and early one Saturday morning the 50-foot, 9' × 27' beams were set. It took all that the 25-ton crane could do. The operator said, "Watch my front wheels. If they lift off the ground, let me know, because then I'll have to drop the beam and drive over to the other side and lift up that end." It was a tense moment as he extended the hydraulic beam out, and out some more, to set the furthest south beam. But he made it, taking only an hour to set all three beams. And then we could walk across the Pequea Creek! It was an historic moment.

Cousin Sam planned a work day on a Saturday in August for his Maryland cousins to come, the Sam R. boys. The three of them and their in-laws came. They placed the cross beams, made forms, and positioned the R-bars. I took a day off from work so we could pour the deck. It took about 16 yards of concrete. We worked late, troweling it and making a broom finish—and at last the bridge could be used. Cousins Sam and Chester made a nice railing out of steel pipe and painted it black to make the bridge look more finished. The total cost of the project was about $10,000.00.

Sure was a great day for Uncle's family, who could now go out the back lane and over the new bridge. They no longer had to use the lane that emptied onto Route 30 and be reminded of the accident which took Uncle's life just 200 feet west of their driveway.

One Sunday morning as we headed out to church, we drove through the fields over to Uncle's farm. We wanted to mark this moment in history by driving over the new bridge on our way to church, and I wanted to show my wife and family our handiwork.

Testing

How much weight could the bridge support? Hoover Steel figured out it could easily carry 10 tons. One day the milkman crossed the bridge in a 40-ton milk truck without seeming to stress the bridge, but otherwise we kept heavy trucks off the bridge.

There were several floods, but the bridge withstood them well. Today, more than 40 years later, it feels satisfying to see the bridge built by farm boys still serving well. The bridge never had an official name, but a fitting title would be Sylvan's Crossing, in memory of Uncle Sylvan who died in 1976 at age 57.

CHAPTER EIGHT

Uncle Joe's Train Wreck in 1928

Engineer Joe Fisher leaned out of the cab window, both arms on the windowsill, and looked back to the Paoli, Pennsylvania, station platform. He was watching the last passengers board his train, the westbound Spirit of St Louis. After loading the baggage, the red caps slammed the baggage car door shut, and the mail clerk stepped back, having just completed taking in the mail.

With a mighty, "All aboard," the conductor gave Joe the signal to move out. Joe pulled the whistle cord with one hand, giving two short toots. He tugged at the throttle and slowly released the brakes. Giving the engine more throttle and less brakes, Joe let the 12-car train pull out, smoke billowing, steam shooting out of the cylinder cocks.

The 48-year-old engineer settled back, his hand latching out the throttle as the engine picked up speed. The 4,000 horsepower, K-4 steam locomotive soon was traveling at 50 miles per hour. On the left-hand side, the fireman watched the stoker jets, keeping an eye on the boiler's water level and the steam gauge.

The K-4 steam locomotives the Pennsy used in those days were the most modern power in their time. They had power reverse, a stoker, and electric lights. They could handle a 12-car passenger train with ease. These were the Pennsylvania Railroad's glory days, when it was the largest railroad in the world. They stabled over 6,000 locomotives, 1,800 passenger cars, and more than 60,000 freight cars. They had over 24,000 miles of track and employed one-tenth of the nation's work force.

Filling the water tank

Joe's train zipped through the mainline towns outside of Philadelphia: Malvern, Exton, Whitford, and Downingtown. Soon the steam engine needed to take on water. Joe reduced the speed to 30 mph, and when the train reached the Atglen track pans, which were marked by a lighted post, the fireman dropped the water scoop, which scooped up about 5,000 gallons of water out of the trough between the rails and forced it into the water tank through a special square chute made in the tender's frame.

Another marker indicated the end of the trough, and the fireman pulled the lever to move the scoop up. Joe reached up, latched out the three-foot-long throttle lever, and slowly released the brakes. The train took off like a runaway mule.

Joe had about 12 years of engineering behind him. Running this Harrisburg-New York line twice a week, he knew the tracks better than his own house. Every curve, every crossing, station stop, and turnout were etched in his mind.

Joe and his fireman usually worked together as a team. They had to know the engine almost better than they knew their wives. How did it steam? At what setting must the stoker be? Could the feed water pump be depended on, or must the injectors be used? Were the flues all open?

When trouble developed, such as bad coal, wet tracks, plugged flues, or sticky brakes, the engineer and fireman had to work together to correct the problem. Each engine and each train handled differently. Each run had its slow orders, and opposing trains could slow things in a hurry. Joe used to tell my dad that if he didn't like the fireman, he could just pull the throttle wide open and laugh at the poor fire boy trying to keep up the steam.

The train shot through Coatesville, Parkesburg, and Atglen. Near Christiana, Joe set the throttle back so the train would slow to 50 mph for the two sharp curves through Gap. Joe had special places along the track marked in his mind—a rock or a fence post or a building where he would set the brakes and reduce the throttle to prepare to slow down or to make a station stop.

After running at 85 mph for 30 miles, the 50 mph through Gap seemed like a crawl. Joe eased off the brakes and kept the throttle open slightly. The train was now coasting downhill toward Leaman Place.

It was the roaring '20's, and the U.S. economy was at an all-time high. Calvin Coolidge was in his second term as president. Joe was also in his prime. He had recently purchased the farm along Route 772 where the Stoltzfus Meat Market would be located, just east of Intercourse. And he had just married Margaret Keener, his childhood sweetheart. Margaret's dad, Pete Keener, had worked for Joe's father, Joel Fisher, as a farmhand. Joe had reasons to feel content.

Catching the railroad bug

Joe was my grandmother's brother. Their parents were Joel and Elizabeth Fisher. Joe was born January 21, 1880, the seventh child in a family of 11. Joel Fishers lived at 2655 Bachmantown Road, southwest of Ronks, when Joe was born. When Joe was five years old, his parents moved to Kansas on a special train. Joe spent some time in the steam locomotive cab on that trip. In 1887, the family moved back, also by train. Again, Joe spent some time in the cab, and it's said that he operated some of the controls. That's when he got the railroad bug.

Joe and his own family eventually moved to a farm just east of Gordonville, but he always hired tenant farmers to do the farm work because he was employed by the railroad. He had started working on the Pennsy Railroad in 1899, when he was 19.

Soon after Joe became an engineer, the route he especially loved became known as the Harrisburg-New York line. He liked to run fast and could make up lost time in almost any circumstance. He soon became known as the "Flying Dutchman," probably a reference to his Amish background.

Back in the Pullman cars, porters were making up the upper and lower berths. The dining car gave its last call for dinner, and passengers finished up their evening meal. In the last car, the 85-foot lounge, folks were exchanging gossip, while others were making new friends. Several well-dressed men discussed the stock market. All were unaware that engineer Joe would soon place the train in a high risk position and lose the gamble.

Red lights and a bouncing box car

Joe rounded the curve at Leaman Place and began to latch out the throttle. The fireman sped up the stoker, anticipating the seven-mile upgrade into Lancaster. The stack roared, smoke billowed forward, the Spirit of St Louis leaped over the Pequea Creek. Then Joe saw the red marker lights of a freight train moving through Gordonville on the No. 2 inside track, about half a mile ahead of Joe's engine. As Joe passed the Gordonville Cemetery, he drew even with the caboose, his headlights outlining the box cars and refrigerator cars on his left. This was a fast freight train also on a fast schedule.

As Joe's train leaned around the 30° curve between Gordonville and Irishtown, he saw what railroad men dread: a wildly bouncing box car. Apparently a broken wheel or a bearing had caused the car to bounce along. It was being held upright by the couplers, or maybe by the truck sliding along on the rails. At any second, the car could break loose and spill over onto Joe's track, causing a serious problem.

Taking an informed chance

Joe had to make a decision—either to drop back and not put his two million dollar train and approximately 200 passengers at great risk, or speed up so he could warn the freight train engineer of the situation, get ahead of a possible derailment, stay on schedule, and be a sudden hero.

Joe chose the more dashing solution. He latched out the throttle, rang the bell, and pulled on the whistle cord. The train's speed picked up quickly as it shot through the three Irishtown grade crossings. He could see the freight engine about 25 car lengths ahead.

Joe did more whistling and blinked the headlight as both trains whipped through Ronks, leaning into the S-curve to the right.

Back in the Pullmans, the well-to-do were still in the lounge enjoying nightcaps and visiting with fellow passengers. In those days the Pennsy had heavyweight Pullmans, weighing over 110 tons each, each with three axle trucks, thick concrete floors, and thick steel walls to provide a quiet comfortable ride. Probably only the most observant passengers noticed the freight train on their left as the Spirit sped through the night. They had no reason to think that the train wouldn't reach St Louis as advertised. Both trains ducked under Beilers' iron bridge and entered the 14-mile stretch before the village of Bird-in-Hand.

Suddenly, the bold Flying Dutchman lost his gamble. The belligerent box car, now just ahead of Joe's engine, broke loose from the freight train. Train cars piled up, spilling over into Joe's path, derailing the Spirit's engine but not upsetting any of its cars. In a flash, Joe's right hand applied the brakes, his left hand shut off the throttle, and both trains came to a screeching stop just south of Bird-in-Hand.

One can only surmise what went through Joe's brain as he called the Harrisburg dispatcher to send out a wrecker, and reached out to another engine to pull the Spirit of St. Louis backwards to Atglen, where it would be switched onto the No. 4 track so it could continue on its now very late schedule.

Here was Joe in the prime of his railroad career, now with a sizable black mark on his record. My dad said he was suspended for 90 days and dropped from Number 3 to Number 10 on the seniority list. All because he took his Flying Dutchman risk and lost.

Joe retired from the railroad in 1946. He died in 1955 and is buried at Heller's Evangelical Reformed Church near Leola.

As you've likely guessed, I've constructed much of this tale from reading railroad lore and from some of my own reasoning about what probably happened, but I'd like to extend thanks to several sources:

- My dad, Gid B. Stoltzfus, whose mother was Joe's sister. As a nine-year-old, he recalls his dad coming home from hauling milk from his dairy farm to the Ronks station and telling Grandma, "Joe had a train wreck last night."

- John M. Beiler, born April, 1910, was 18 years old and worked at the Jonas Beiler farm on Lynnwood Road near Bird-in-Hand. He recalls walking out to the tracks just behind their farm the next morning and seeing the derailed cars scattered about along the right of way.
- The curator of the Strasburg Railroad Museum for the 1928 Pennsylvania Railroad schedule.

CHAPTER NINE

Slow Orders Through Gordonville

You think there are lots of trains today? Here's a little bit about the train activity I witnessed as I was growing up in the middle of farm country.

"Sammy, quick get up! The trains are going real slow." My mother woke me early that morning in 1953 when I was 10 years old. But what got me up fast was the piercing whistle of a GGI electric locomotive sounding two longs, one short, and one long for the Cherry Lane grade crossing. On went my broadfall trousers. I raced downstairs. Glancing out the west window I saw a slow-moving eastbound varnish passenger train just past the Irishtown crossing. Quickly, I scooted out to the barn to do my chores while *Dat* did the milking. With one eye peeled on the Pennsy four-track, Harrisburg to Philly main line, which stretched across the north horizon from Ronks to Gordonville, I kept wondering why the trains were going so slow?

Out to the meadow I went to feed the chickens, which ran loose those days. Another G's whistle got my attention. Another eastbound varnish was coming out of Ronks, most likely the Clevelander, scheduled for Harrisburg at 4:30 a.m., already an hour late. The first train was probably the Philadelphia Night Express, easy to spot because it had eight to ten mail express cars and two or three day coaches.

The Clevelander clattered along at about 10 miles an hour, blowing for the three grade crossings—Cherry Lane, Irishtown, and Harvest Drive. Then it rounded the curve and disappeared into the cut at Milepost 58.

Again I heard a rumble, and another GGI poked its nose out of Ronks, blowing two longs, one short, and one long for the Cherry Lane crossing.

Normally traveling at 85 miles an hour, hoggers can't blow more than two complete warnings as they zip through the three crossings. Most likely this one was the Cincinnati Limited, due at Harrisburg at 4:47 and at Paoli at 6:12, already a half-hour tardy. The string of varnish went by, steam blowing off from the G on this mild April morning.

What was going on?

Our chores done and now at breakfast, even *Dat*, wise in railroad lore, was mystified about what could be wrong. Just then, another train rumbled through Ronks. It was an express with several coaches on the rear, probably No. 68, the Red Arrow, due in Lancaster at 5:58, also over half an hour behind.

My mind whirled as I hoped these slow-moving trains would continue at least as I walked to school. Quickly I put on my school broadfall trousers, and then off I ran, dashing east on Irishtown Road, which was about 400 yards south of the main line, running pell-mell to Gordonville until I got to Leacock Road, just south of the overpass at Milepost 58.

Another GGI blew for the crossings, a string of Tuscan Red Pullmans tied to its coupling. Slowly it cruised east, probably the Central-Trail Blazer, No. 48, an all-Pullman train out of Chicago. Carded at Harrisburg at 5:06, it was over an hour late.

In 1953, 12 eastbound varnishes passed through Gordonville between 4:30 a.m. and the mail train at 7:45 a.m. This was the morning rush hour. And it was a rush to track side for me. Just as I passed over the Leacock Road bridge, I heard another GGI whistle. Sure enough, there she came, blowing for the crossings, the Liberty Limited, No. 58 from Chicago, already an hour late.

I still enjoy that Grand Pennsy glamour. The two GGIs on point, already 16 years old but still looking young, they pranced along at 10 miles an hour, pushing their long noses through the soft spring morning. Did I just imagine it, or was the hogger straining to hold them back, keeping the reins tight by making a two-pound reduction on the air brakes now and then? Pentographs sizzled; steam blew off the lead G's nose. The long train clattered past, two baggage cars, a string of almost new Tuscan Red Pullmans about six years old, two dining cars, and then more

Pullmans. Finally there was the rounded-end observation car, with the drumhead proudly proclaiming Liberty Limited.

The wheels sounded almost comical clunking over the switch frog at Hoobers Mill. The two-axle trucks went clunk-clunk. Those cars with three axle trucks went chunk-clunk-clunk, clunk-clunk-clunk.

Just as the Liberty Limited disappeared around the curve into the town of Paradise, I heard another whistle in the west—a series of two longs, one short, two long blasts. I waited at the Leacock Road bridge staircase landing alongside the trains. The steps went from the road down to the track level.

Distracted

School had to wait that morning. The next GGI appeared ¼ mile to the west, then purred by, past the mail crane. Percy Troup, the local who hung up the mail bag and took the incoming bag to the Post Office, sat in his little shanty using colorful language to describe the late trains.

The train slipped around the curve into Paradise, over the three-arched stone Pequea Creek bridge, half of which was built in the 1860s, and the second half in 1899. The train moved through Leaman Place. Hopefully it would get to Philly by noon. The drumhead read Indianapolis Limited, which was scheduled to stop in Lancaster at 6:59, but by now it was 45 minutes late.

Another rumble in Ronks and more crossing warnings, this

time with an impatient note, and another pair of GGIs came into view and slowly cruised past. How nice it would have been to see my Great-Uncle Joe in a K-steam engine, bringing his train through Gordonville. Joe worked for the Pennsy Railroad for 46 years—30 some as an engineer, running several crack varnishes, including the Spirit of St. Louis and the Cincinnati Limited.

Already I could see this was a long train. The conductor was in the first Pullman, its top door open, glaring at his 21 Jewel Hamilton, the chain dangling in the breeze, peering front at the fireman, as if that would help make up time.

The fireman waved a hand at me. He was not so busy on this warm morning. Steam was blowing off here and there, steam escaping along the cars. The generator belts could be heard flapping. Then seven Pullmans glided by. I could see potbellied gents in shorts and T-shirts in the roomettes doing their morning shaving. The two-section diner moved by, the smell of flapjacks, eggs, and fried potatoes wafting through the Gordonville breeze.

Pennsy President James M. Symes probably would have frowned at all these crack trains running late, his $750 million investment in passenger train equipment realizing a larger loss. (Pennsy stock last paid dividends in 1946.)

More Pullmans clattered by. In the drawing rooms, couples in their night clothes peered out at this Amish schoolboy, likely wondering why they weren't seeing the buildings in the "City of Brotherly Love," which is where they should have been if they were on schedule.

Suddenly I heard the school bell. Oh, my! School! Up Maple Street I dashed, making better time than the trains, ran through the door, tossed my straw hat and black coat on their hook, and slid into my seat. Teacher Mrs. Reynolds glared at me. While saluting the flag, I heard more GGI whistles, probably No. 30, the Spirit of St Louis, cruising by, carded for Lancaster at 7:23 a.m., over 45 minutes late.

Mail bag pick-up and delivery

It was hard to concentrate on school lessons as I heard more whistles. Another train clattered by, most likely the Fort Pitt, which had an RPO (Railway Post Office) car tucked behind the GGI. I saw it zip through town many times at 7:45 a.m. As it neared the mail crane, the engineer would toot the whistle, the RPO car door would open, the mail bag hook would fold out and catch the hanging bag, and the pistol-toting mail clerk on the train would toss out the outgoing bag. Percy Troop would hustle out of his shanty, pick up the mail bag, muttering his colorful words, and head off to the Gordonville Post Office. "*Wie bish, Bova*" (How are you, boy?), he'd holler to me, the only Pennsylvania Dutch he knew.

Probably this morning the RPO clerks had all the time in the world to hook the bag. They could have *handed* the outgoing bag to Percy as the train glided past.

During first recess I looked southeast toward Paradise at signal bridge 591 and saw the two eastbound signal lights in a horizontal position, which meant "stop." At noon the lights were in a vertical position, so they were operating again.

What happened that made these trains run with such restraint? They were running about like the first trains through here in 1834, when this was the one-track Philadelphia and Columbia Railway. Then 70 percent of the trains were horse-drawn.

The next day one of the Pennsy employees' children (several lived in town) brought the official report: some thieves stole signal wires in Parkesburg (12 miles to the east), thus shutting down the signal system from the cork tower at the Lancaster train station to the Atglen tower where the A&S branch met the main line. The signals went dark, so the trains had slow orders for safety reasons.

The next morning, the Limiteds ran on time, whooshing through Gordonville at 85 miles an hour. The GGIs were in full stride, and I got to school at the proper time.

CHAPTER TEN

Cowboy Sailors

Soon after World War II was over, the U.S. government and Mennonite Central Committee (a North American relief and service agency which the Amish sometimes work with; often referred to as "MCC") decided to help war-torn Germany, China, and Japan get on their feet again. They decided to send them horses, heifers, and goats by the ship-load. Of course this required lots of help, including loading the animals and then caring for them on the long voyage across the ocean. Amish and Mennonite farm boys who were experienced in animal care got involved.

My father would tell of the time in late 1946 when his former hired man signed up to go along with a boatload of 800 heifers to China. This was quite an adventure for a farm lad who had never gone far from home, let alone by boat.

The sea-going cowboys had to take care of some legal and medical requirements. First, they had to join the Merchant Marines in Baltimore, and then get Social Security numbers, which no Amish had back then. Each one needed four vaccinations and a strict physical. They had to get their pictures taken and be fingerprinted. All who were draft age had to have their draft board's permission to leave the country, and those under 18 had to have written parental permission. The Merchant Marines required a swearing-in process. However, the Plain folks were permitted to say "I affirm," rather than "I swear."

In November of 1943, representatives from 44 countries had met at the White House and formed the United Nations Relief and Rehabilitation Administration (UNRRA). Its first shipment of cattle was in March, 1945—six bulls bound for Greece. In June, 1945, a shipment of 588 horses left New Orleans for Greece. So the project got started. In all, UNRRA had 73 livestock ships crossing the oceans. From June, 1945 through 1947, over 7,000 cowboy sailors were involved.

Some 20,000 animals—heifers, horses, bulls, and goats—were shipped to Japan, Greece, central Europe, and China. The families that received these animals were very grateful. In many cases, the animals' offspring were kept in the families' living quarters. Over three billion donated dollars were spent to ship the animals.

Adventure for farm boys

In early December of 1946, 20 boys—three Amish and 17 Mennonite lads—were told to report to Newport News, Virginia, with their bags packed for the trip to China. In due time, 800 heifers were chased aboard a 400-foot-long Victory ship. These ships were World War II freighters whose three lower decks had been converted into cattle pens.

Lines were cast off, and the boat headed out to the open sea, taking the boys on an adventure they wouldn't soon forget. The boat turned south along the coastline, sailed across the Gulf of Mexico, and then through the Panama Canal. The boys soon developed their ship routine for feeding and watering the heifers. These boys were accustomed to livestock and knew what heifers would eat. However, their shipboard supervisor insisted that the boys feed the hay as he dictated. But the heifers didn't eat it all.

Then just as they were passing through the Panama Canal, the ship's boilers gave out. There was nothing to do but wait. Because there was no power, there was no electricity and no ventilation in the lower decks for the animals. More than 100 heifers perished. The dead animals had to be pulled up three decks by block and tackle and chucked overboard.

Pausing in California

At first, another ship towed the cattle boat for a day or so, and then a canal tugboat took over and pulled the cattle boat to Long Beach, California. All of this took two weeks. In California the heifers were unloaded and trucked to nearby pastures. Meanwhile, it took another two weeks or so to repair the boilers. So the boys cleaned out the pens, and then to pass the time, they rented a car and toured the countryside.

Finally the boilers were repaired, the heifers were reloaded, and the long voyage across the Pacific began. Seven days a week the shipboard routine was the same: eat breakfast, feed the heifers, water the heifers. The boys played lots of pinochle. And there were storms, sometimes with waves higher than the boat. However, through storms and fair weather, the boat docked at Shanghai, China.

These Victory ships were under the administration of the U.S. Marine Maritime Commission from 1943 through 1946. Five hundred thirty-four were built. They were 455 feet long, almost as long as average corn rows, and 62 feet wide, about as wide as a barn is long. They drew 28 feet of water and could haul 10,850 tons. Their top speed was 18.5 miles an hour, the speed of a very fast horse. They were powered by steam turbines. A crew of 90 men was needed to operate the ship at sea. The boats that hauled animals had three decks built in their cargo holds. The pens were made of heavy oak timbers. Hay and grain were stored on each deck or on the top deck.

In January of 1947, the heifers were unloaded, and then the ship's long journey back across the Pacific began. Since the boat was now empty, it rode high in the water. During storms it rolled dangerously, so much that the boys wondered if they would see their homeland again. Finally the four-month journey was over. The 20 boys were given their pay—$200.00 each, plus $60.00 each for train fare home. The Merchant Marine pay was one cent a month.

Two lads hitchhiked home to Ontario, Canada, and beat two

others who traveled by bus. The Amish boys traveled by train and arrived home in Lancaster County in late March.

I can recall it like yesterday when our hired man came home. He came walking across the meadow, right up behind my dad and grandpa, and gave them each a big slap on the back. There was lots of talking and laughing as we greeted the hired man who had come home again.

CHAPTER ELEVEN

Wheat Threshing Time with Joe and His Steam Engine

When I was a young Amish boy, it was considered a sin to let straw leave the farm instead of using it for bedding. With its seed head harvested, the remaining wheat stalk was useful in the cow stable. In those days, every farmer in Lancaster County, Pennsylvania grew wheat, a moneymaker at $2.25 a bushel.

Wheat was important not just as a cash crop and for the straw, but because farmers believed it was a soil purifier. Every four years, many farmers planted it on one-quarter of their tillable acreage. Year One—wheat; Year Two—hay; Year Three—corn; Year Four—tobacco and corn; then wheat again.

Threshing time!

In 1949, my dad, my uncle Sylvan, and a neighbor named Pete put their money together and bought a wooden, 24-inch Frick threshing machine. They made a cross-shaft and pulleys to hook the thresher onto Pete's McCormick 50T baler. That allowed the baler, powered by a long belt, to be placed behind the thresher. Baled straw fit into a much smaller space than loose straw, ensuring that no straw left the farm.

After World War II, when most of the English farmers in the area were buying combines, many used threshers came on the market. That's when Amish farmers formed simple companies of three, four, or five farmers and bought their own threshers and tractors.

I was about seven when we got our thresher. What a marvelous machine it was! In my small-boy's world, it looked big and complicated, with belts and pulleys everywhere, small lids to open and look inside, and a step to crawl up and over. During rainy days that spring, Uncle Sylvan and Pete came over to get the threshing machine ready. Fix this, tighten that, replace the worn belts, and oil and grease every bearing.

Threshing season was a happy time. When the wheat was bright yellow, *Dat* would say, *"Sis tresha zeit!"* (It's threshing time!) Then he'd get out the binder and cut the wheat. Next, he and our hired man, Dave, shocked the wheat, making nice rows across the field. It was the highlight of summer—a kind of

Super Bowl of agriculture as farmers all over the neighborhood got ready to thresh.

Local mills put on extra help and hired more trucks to haul wheat. Hoober's Mill in Gordonville loaded 30 to 40 boxcars of wheat at their rail siding in one season. I can still see *Dat's* satisfied face when he got his wheat check.

We had about 15 acres of wheat, our farm's quota. Because *Dat*, Uncle Sylvan, and neighbor Pete didn't have extra money to buy a tractor, they hired Joe King and his Frick steam engine to come power the threshing machine.

Joe, a confirmed bachelor, was about 45. He bought his Frick steam engine in late 1940 and steamed tobacco beds every spring. His steamer had a $9\frac{1}{2}'' \times 10''$ cylinder, so Joe referred to it simply as "my $9\frac{1}{2}$ by 10." It seemed his steamer was kind of like his wife. He cleaned, oiled, and fussed with it, paying as much attention to the steamer as other men paid to their wives. Joe would drive his big monster up our barn hill and back it onto thick planks so it would sit level. The steamer had to be level to keep the water in its boiler level.

The thresher was set up in the barn, with its long belt running out through the barn door to the steamer pulley. When a load of wheat sheaves was hauled into the barn, Joe blew the whistle with two short toots and then hollered in his screechy voice, "Fingers out!"

Slowly the steamer started. Its belt flapped and slipped some, but soon the thresher was running. As the process got under way, someone always said, *"Na sin mah un dresha!"* (Now we're threshing!) It was such an exciting thing to watch from the wheat bags where my two sisters and I sat. It didn't matter how much noise and dust there was, we stayed for hours.

When we finally did tire, my one sister and I moved outside to watch Joe and his steamer. Joe fiddled with this and that adjustment and shoveled coal into the firebox. When he stopped the engine, he turned the grease cups up a bit to force grease into the bearings. Whenever he had a free moment, he wiped and cleaned his machine.

A community project

In 1951, I began going along with *Dat* to help thresh at Uncle Sylvan's and Pete's farms. In the early morning, *Dat* hitched Doll and Bess to the wagon, and the horses pulled us, rattling along through the field lanes. As we went, we could see to the north that Ike King, a custom thresher, was set up at one of his places. To the west, Becky Fisher's boys had their rig set up in one of their fields. We said to each other, *"All die leit war un dresha!"* (All the folks are threshing!)

By the time we got to Uncle's or Pete's, the two of them were already greasing and fussing with the thresher and baler. And Joe would be firing up his steamer. He usually slept in the barn and cleaned the flues first thing each morning. Steamers weren't like tractors, which were ready to go with just a few good cranks. It took an hour to get the steam pressure up to 160 pounds. Joe only had time for a quick breakfast before getting back to work the steamer's fire. Whenever he ate in a farmhouse, he left soot and grease marks on the bench and table, which didn't make the woman of the household very happy.

Joe's last firing

But one year on a Saturday night, Joe's romance with the steam engine ended. Our crop and Uncle's crop had been finished, and there was one load to go before completing Pete's. It was about dark, and the men were determined to finish up the job that evening. But Joe's firing fell short—he hadn't kept the boiler hot enough to finish that last load.

Dat always said Joe was afraid of his steamer and not the best fireman. If Joe was overly cautious, it was because of all the tales of steamers blowing up. That night the men had to quit, then come back again Monday to finish the load at Pete's. From then on, Uncle fired the steamer and Joe worked in the field. About 1953, *Dat*, Uncle, and Pete got a Hart Parr tractor, so they didn't need Joe King's steamer anymore.

When there wasn't any work on farms like ours, Joe worked for Art Young Equipment in Kinzers, cleaning and repairing steam engines and replacing flues and grates. If there was dirty work to do, Joe did it. His skin was almost the color of grease.

Most of his life he lived with his many cats in a small, two-room house converted from a chicken coop. He had huge pockets in his broadfall pants. Eyewitnesses said those pockets were known to simultaneously hold three cans of cat food, a loaf of bread, several packs of chewing tobacco, some small tools, and a little loose change. I recall once seeing Joe dressed in his Sunday best at a funeral, and I barely recognized him.

When he wasn't working, Joe often went fishing. At one point, he had a small boat. He helped thresh in Lancaster County until 1959 or so, and died in 1973.

Despite the importance wheat once had to farmers in Lancaster County, the number of acres planted in wheat slowly declined because of the drop in its price. By 1985, only 10% of county farms grew the crop. Today in 2018, there are only a few farmers in Leacock Township who thresh wheat.

The Amish are prohibited from flying, in an effort to keep their focus on their families, their church, and their local communities. Yet they are accommodating to outsiders who need help, including pilots from the Air Force, even though they do not enter the military for conscience reasons.

Traditionally, Amish wedding season is in the late fall, when the main field work and harvesting are over. Then there is more time for planning and preparing for weddings and enjoying the fellowship that is always a part of them.

CHAPTER TWELVE

The Intercourse Airport

An airport in the Pequea? Well, almost. Back in the fall of 1956, as a young chap of 13, I was up in the silo throwing down corn silage late in the afternoon of October 26. The roaring of a low— really low—flying airplane caused me to drop my fork and look out the silo chute window, just in time to see a two-motor plane go by approximately 100 feet above the silo. I made a new world record crawling down the silo chute, and for the next 10 minutes, *Dat*, my brother John, and I watched the plane frantically circle in the direction of Intercourse, Pennsylvania.

The pilot rapidly circled back and forth, each pass about parallel with Route 340, from just over the area west of Intercourse, almost to Bird-in-Hand. You could sense his urgency to land as darkness neared, rain fell, and fog moved in. Then the plane made one last circle, and we could no longer see it, but we were sure it was behind the Gid Fisher ridge. We heard the engine sputter and stop, a loud bang, and then silence. Minutes later, the Intercourse and Gordonville fire sirens went off. I will never forget the look on *Dat*'s face as he said, "I bet the plane crashed." A lot of people thought the plane would hit their buildings, it had been circling so low.

The next morning we learned from the milkman that a big plane was sitting just west of Sim Kauffman's barn, now the Dan Esh farm on Harvest Drive. At school that day we learned the facts.

The plane, a two-motor, 14-ton, C46 army plane, with Walter Bachman, age 34, as pilot; Thomas Clock, 35, as co-pilot; along with Henry LaRocke, 25, had wanted to land at Olmstead Air Force Base, now the Harrisburg International Airport. But the airport was expecting another plane, which unknown at the time, had crashed in heavy fog near Cumberland, Pennsylvania. So this plane was sent to the Lancaster Airport. But it was closed due to the bad weather. Radios then didn't have the range we're used to, so the crew had no way of knowing beforehand. They were told, "Go find a field and set her down."

When a field becomes a landing strip

The plane groped its way through the fog over Intercourse and frantically searched for a landing place. As it made one last circle, its engine stopped, out of fuel. The plane glided in, caught the electric wires over C.B. Hoobers, and came down, heading in a southwest direction on the top of the hill in Junie Esh's Aaron's field. It skidded halfway across the field, and then the pilot saw a row of trees along Clearview Road. The wires the plane was dragging along behind it proved to be a blessing. It slowed the plane down quite effectively, allowing the pilot to make a quick turn and head south, coasting to a stop in what is now Johnnie Esh's field.

What a relief the crew must have felt to step onto solid ground, the plane in one piece. Thirty-four-year-old pilot Walter Bachman had set her down in a field that was only one-third the length of the runway it was accustomed to using for landing. Yonie Esh's Amie and the hired girl were husking corn in the field at the time and had huddled under the farm wagon.

Well, the fire trucks came, but when there was no fire, they went home. The electric company worked half the night to fix the wires, and military police from Olmstead guarded the plane.

Making a runway

The following day, plans were made to fly the plane out again. Air Force personnel trucked in a crew and brought a heavy roller to make as smooth a runway as possible. They took down the meadow fences and electric wires along Harvest Drive, and then graded and rolled an 1800-foot runway from the top of the hill down to Harvest Drive.

And then it rained for two days straight. The runway was too soggy to use. Meanwhile, Ike Eisenhower won his second bid for President of the United States. The Amish talked about the upcoming weddings. We young folks were caught up in how the Yankees had beaten the Dodgers in the just-past World Series. (Don Larsen had pitched a perfect game that year, remember?)

Then the weather turned nice, the soggy fields dried out, and on the morning of November 4, 1956, as I arrived at the Intercourse Elementary School, we heard that the plane would be taking off that day. It was very hard to concentrate on our lessons. About 9:00, helicopters arrived from Olmstead, about 40 miles away. They brought the crew that would fly the plane out. As they circled over the schoolyard, history and spelling were forgotten.

The action was over by Clearview Road. The teachers let us go out in the schoolyard to see what we could see. The take-off field was about a half-mile away across town, so we really couldn't see much.

The story goes that Major Ed L. Thompson and Captain

Donald Hawks were the crew, test pilots from Olmstead. They started the engines and taxied the plane north to the top of the hill. The pilot turned it south and slowly made a test trip down over the field.

Remember, in those days there were not big jets that covered a half-acre, that could haul 250 people or six cattle trucks full of cows. The biggest planes then were a D.C. 7 and a B29 bomber, that had 150-foot wingspans, about as wide as 50 36"-wide corn rows.

This aircraft, a Curtiss C-46 Commando Military Transport version of the CW-20 had a wing span of 108 feet and was 76 feet, four inches long, weighed 14 tons empty, and could carry 17,336 pounds.

Its cruising speed was about 200 miles per hour. Its passenger capacity was about 50 persons. It was first developed in 1940. A total of 3,182 were built.

Back at the Intercourse "Airport," Major Ed slowly turned his plane 180 degrees and taxied back north across the dirt runway to the top of the hill and turned again, facing south. It was a beautiful November day with a clear sky. Clearview Road was lined with farmers and neighbors. They filled the lawns, porch roofs, and low barn roofs. Corn-husking and fodder-shocking were forgotten; wedding preparations waited. This was a major event. A big plane was taking off in the neighborhood.

The mechanics walked around the plane one more time and checked it over carefully. Then they gave Major Ed the go-ahead.

He set the brakes, revved up the engine to its take-off speed, then quickly released the brakes. This gave him a little more speed, sort of like backing up the horses, and then slamming into the traces.

Slowly the plane started its ascent, gradually picking up speed. The people watching held their breaths. The plane had already covered half the runway when its tail lifted, the engines revved up to their limits, and the exhaust flamed. But did the wheels leave the ground?

Thanking the "hosts"

Yes, the plane was in the air, already about 100 feet away from Harvest Drive. Clearing the road by five feet, the plane headed south, gaining altitude. When it had nearly reached Belmont Road, it turned left, making a big circle right over the schoolyard where 120 of us school children watched. Now the plane was about 1500 feet up in the air. The pilot dipped the wings; then away he went, off in a northerly direction toward Middletown, his destination airport.

Sometime soon after the plane landed in the field, a local jokester put up a sign at the intersection of Route 340 and Clearview Road. It read "Intercourse Airport, flight now leaving," with an arrow pointing south toward where the plane had sat. A crew came and replaced fences, the farmers re-sowed their fields, and the sign fell over. Life in the Pequea was back to normal.

CHAPTER THIRTEEN

The Woman and the Baby in the Snowstorm

Anna Buckwalter, now 100 years old, had in her earlier years been a Lancaster county taxi driver for the Amish. On the evening of January 28, 1977, her kitchen clock said 5:15. The slightly plump, 60-some-years-young woman moved about in the delicious smelling kitchen, preparing the evening meal. Just as she turned the fried potatoes, the phone rang. "Oh my!" she thought, "Hope it's not an urgent matter." All afternoon the radio had been blaring a storm-watch report.

The voice on the phone was in a hurry and went straight to the point: "Anna, could you take me and our two-day-old daughter to the Osteopathic Hospital. Dr. Kaiser was just here and said she is turning yellow and needs to be admitted right away and put under the blue light."

On call

"Who is this?" Anna asked, a frown forming on her face, her hair turning just a shade more gray. "Sam Stoltzfus, Mill Lane, Gordonville."

Without the slightest hesitation she said, "I'll be right there."

She turned off the burner, grabbed her bag and coat, put on her bonnet, flew out the door, backed her blue Ford station wagon out the drive, and sped away. Little did she realize it would be 16 or so hours before she would set foot back in her own kitchen.

After a two-mile, six-minute trip, she arrived at the white house on Mill Road. Large black clouds were already darkening the sun, and snow flurries were coming out of the northwest. The sky had the makings of a big thunderstorm, but there were also cold and snow in those clouds.

Wearing his black hat and heavy overcoat, the father came hurrying out the walks, carrying the little bundle wrapped in blankets, and got into the car. The rest of his family—his wife, two boys, and two small girls—were waving goodbye as the baby's mother called after her husband, "Keep the blankets over her face."

As the blue Ford rolled out the lane, the storm hit. Big

snowflakes plastered the windshield, and the sky grew very dark. The winds were blowing at 30 to 40 miles an hour.

"You know, Anna," the father spoke up, "why don't we have the ambulance take us to the hospital? Then you can go home. It's really going to storm."

Anna replied, "I'll say yes to that."

"Then take us to the firehouse."

"Where's the firehouse?"

"Turn left here, go over the railroad, and turn right," Sam answered.

By now the windshield wipers could hardly keep the snow away. Anna held a tight grip on the steering wheel, while her face was set in a worried frown. But she was strong and determined. The 20-second drive to the firehouse took six minutes. The call for an ambulance was made. One of the ambulance personnel, 60-year-old Mrs. Mays, took the baby, while her husband, Paul, got behind the wheel. Another responder climbed into the co-pilot's seat, and the baby's father sat in the middle of the back seat.

Anna bravely backed her wagon away from the firehouse and steered south on Leacock Road. The storm had intensified greatly by now. Big globs of falling snow, a howling wind, bone-chilling cold, and already three inches of wet snow made the roads extremely treacherous. This Arctic Circle snowstorm had started in the Midwest that morning.

Sheer grit

Anna turned her car 90 degrees west onto Irishtown Road. Visibility was now near zero as she drove directly into the storm. Never in her 30 years of taxi business had she been in such a tempest. Breathing a silent prayer while gently pressing on the accelerator, her foot ready to hit the brake, and with a good hold on the steering wheel, she bravely handled the situation calmly. She was alone in the storm, much like Lindbergh over the Atlantic, but in the presence of a higher power.

She crawled slowly along from one street light to the next until she was out of Gordonville. Then she drove by guess and by golly, hoping the next telephone pole would be beside her instead of looming up between the headlights. Past Kinsinger's barn she advanced ever so slowly, then past the Stoltzfus lane. Where's that curve ahead? And where are those culverts? She flipped the headlight beams up and down, spotted the next pole, and then began looking for the T road off to Soudersburg. Which way should I go, she wondered? Then, I'll take the Irishtown Road to Ronks because it's probably open.

Up ahead on the left at the old Stoltzfus homestead, 58-year-old Sarah and her 90-year-old mother, Fannie Stoltzfus, were spending a quiet evening together. Sarah had been out to fetch some milk, and as she came in, stomping snow off her boots, said, "It's not fit for a dog to be out." Then her eyes caught a glimpse of headlights. "Well, there's a car coming up the road."

Anna was able to pull her car off the road at the Stoltzfus home and decided to stay right there until morning. When she knocked on the door, she was welcomed into a warm room and given a recliner to spend the night. Her husband, John, was off in another county and had not planned to return that night, so he wasn't home worrying about her.

The Stoltzfus home had once been a wayside inn, as Anna remembered, "So there was room at the inn for me that stormy, never-to-be-forgotten night!"

The ambulance made it to the hospital, where the baby was well cared for and survived and is now a healthy woman in her early forties.

From that night on, her father Sam had a new name in Anna Buckwalter's memory—"Snowstorm Sam!"

CHAPTER FOURTEEN

Taking *Doddys* to Church

Back in the 1960s, about the time I turned 16, my grandfather Sam suffered a stroke. He was in his 80s and lost the use of his left hand. With lots of therapy, he was able to do a little carpentry work, which was his profession. But he could no longer drive his horse. So I was appointed to drive him and *Mommy* to church.

In those days, our family lived on a 75-acre dairy farm in a rambling, two-story, two-unit farm house. Our family, which at that time included eight girls and four boys, lived in one unit. Our grandparents and 46-year-old, single Aunt Liz lived in the *Doddyhaus*.

We Amish have worship services every two weeks in members' homes. Our church district was long and narrow, and we often had to drive six to nine miles, depending upon who was hosting the worship service that day.

The Sunday morning routine was always the same. About 6:00 in the morning, *Mommy* would come over to our kitchen and ask, *"Kann der Sammy mit uns in die Gmay geh?"* Which is

Pennsylvania Dutch for, "Can Sammy go with us to church?"

"Sure," *Dat* would say as he dug into his Sunday morning breakfast. Then he'd glance up at me at the other end of the table, and I'd say, "Sure."

Of course, it was assumed that this was my job—or privilege—as *Mam* would gently remind me. "Do it gladly so that when you're an old grandpappy, your grandchildren will take you to church," she'd say.

Dressed in his Sunday best

When I was little, I had fun riding to church with our grandparents. Because our family was too large for all of us to ride together in our carriage, two of us kids always went with them. Usually it was the two siblings who *Mam* determined had been the best behaved the previous two weeks.

I must admit though, that I became less excited about this so-called privilege when I became the driver and began dating my girlfriend, who later became my wife. The prospect of getting up early to take my grandparents to church kept me from staying out as late as I would have liked on Saturday nights.

But on Sunday mornings, I'd quickly fork down my breakfast of eggs, shoofly, and cereal. Then I'd dash upstairs and put on my Sunday best—black broadfall pants, freshly ironed white shirt, black jacket and coat, shiny black shoes, and my black hat.

Then I'd head to the barn where *Doddy* was already brushing and currying his horse Silver as best as he could with his right hand. Silver was an old sorrel, rather slow, but gentle. A good grandfather horse.

Doddy looked quite dignified in his black Sunday suit—a big contrast from the nail bag and hammer he had strapped around his waist during the week. "Silver is always so hairy," he'd mutter. That would soon be followed by "*Mommy* is always in a hurry to go early."

Meanwhile, *Mommy* and Aunt Liz would push the carriage out of the shed and put blankets inside. Then *Doddy* and I would hitch up Silver, and about the time we were ready to go, one of my little brothers or sisters would dash out and sit with *Mommy* and Liz in the back seat.

Doddy and I would climb into the front seat, with me on the right-hand driver's side. "Giddyap," and we were off. Now you've guessed that I wasn't going with my grandparents. They were going with me!

Mommy's unwritten rules

On this particular morning, we were headed to the Beilers' house, which was at the far southern end of our district. So we left a bit earlier than usual. "There go Amos U's!" *Mommy* exclaimed. Among her unwritten church-going rules was that we should never arrive at church before Amos U's because Amos was our oldest preacher, but always before Dave P's, some of our other senior members.

We cruised south on Soudersburg Road and crossed Route 30. There was hardly any traffic. Along the way, *Doddy* recalled his old days of carpentry. "In 1948 I helped build Sam Fisher's barn over there," he'd say. "Over here, I built Lizzie's house in 1946."

Silver puttered along at his usual slow gait. I'd have much rather driven my shiny black horse Lester, who was much faster.

As we crossed the Herr Mill two-span covered bridge, *Mommy* looked back and saw that we were ahead of Dave P's. This pleased her to no end. "*Die weibsleit sin verdechdich,*" *Doddy* muttered, which means, "These women are funny."

We cruised south on Paradise Lane, a pleasant drive. Somehow, the Sunday morning air seemed more holy, and there were blessings all around.

By now a string of horses and carriages were behind us. The hoof beats on the blacktop made a pretty rhythm. Old horses plodded along. Younger horses almost pranced, their heads up and ears twitching.

Doddy talks politics

Doddy's conversation turned to politics. His memory must have held several encyclopedias, and this morning he talked long and loud about Roosevelt and Eisenhower.

Born in 1882, he was able to recall Grover Cleveland, not to mention Harrison, Teddy Roosevelt, Taft, Harding, Coolidge, and Hoover. He'd talk again and again in great detail about

McKinley's assassination and Woodrow Wilson and World War II, so that you'd think he was their next-door neighbor. As a staunch Republican, he didn't express much favor for Kennedy or Johnson though.

We headed south to Route 741, then drove east a bit and south to the Beilers' lane. We let *Mommy* and Aunt Liz off at the house, then drove out to the barn and unhitched. By now, many other carriages had arrived, and *Doddy* was shaking hands all around.

I put Silver away and found a comfortable hay bale where I could sit and take a short nap. We were early, and it would be 20 minutes before any of the other boys arrived.

At 8:20, we all marched into the house, shook hands with the ministers, took our seats, and the worship service began. At 11:30, the service was over, and we ate dinner. And by 12:30, we were on our way home again.

I'm a grandfather myself now, and I often think of those special Sunday mornings way back then. It certainly seems that life was less complicated then, and I yearn for those slower-paced times.

Silver is long gone. *Doddy* died in 1971. Aunt Liz married in 1972. But the happy memories remain of going to church with *Doddy* and *Mommy*. Or did they go with me?

*By providing a **Doddyhaus** for the grandparents on a farm, usually operated primarily by their son and his wife and family, three generations can live near each other. The older couple can continue to be involved in work on the farm as they wish, but without bearing the full responsibility. Grandchildren and grandparents learn to know each other well and benefit from each other's lives.*

CHAPTER FIFTEEN

Life on Our Farm: Several Grandchildren's Views (from a few years ago)

My name is Daniel. I'm 4 years old. I spend most of my time just watching what happens on our farm where I live with my brothers and sisters, my parents, my uncles, and my grandparents. We all see each other a lot. Most of the time I play with my toys. Out in the barn I have a little red scooter. When it's sunny and warm I play in the sandbox with my sister Sylvia and cousin Sam D. Often we play in *Doddy* Sam's shop. It's long and wide. We can scoot all over the place if *Doddy* isn't making a shed or gazebo in the big part of the shop.

Doddy and *Mommy* live in the *Doddyhaus* end of our big farm house. My parents, Gideon and Leah, and all of my sisters and brothers and I live in the farm house end. My dad, Gideon, tends the 48 cows and does the farming—plowing, planting, and harvesting the crops from the 40 acres.

Every morning at 7:00 or so, *Doddy* goes scurrying out his and *Mommy*'s front door. He often has a tea mug in hand as he quickly walks out to his shop. Soon the diesel starts, and *Doddy* is banging away in his woodworking shop, making a shed, gazebo, or cabinets. Often cousin Sam D. and I get some nails, sneak *Doddy*'s hammer, and pound them into a scrap 2 × 4. Sometimes we hit our fingers. Ouchie! But mostly we're having fun, until *Doddy* sees us, and then he says, "Grrr," and there goes our hammer. At times I get my scooter and zip through the shop, right under *Doddy*'s nose. Then *Doddy* says "Grrr," too!

About every two weeks or so, *Doddy* goes over to his horseradish cooler and pulls out two bags of horseradish roots, plops them onto his big blue express wagon, takes them over to his shop, and sorts them. Then he chops them into pieces. After they're washed, *Mommy*, Uncle Ike, and Uncle Elmer go over the roots and cut out any black spots. *Doddy* puts the cleaned, trimmed roots through the grinder in his little horseradish room in the shop. I don't watch long because it smells funny in there. Once *Doddy* said, *"Steck die nass in dea kivel."* (Stick your nose in this bucket.) I did it, and whew, such a strong horseradish smell. Tears came to my eyes and I ran away crying. *Doddy* did pity me a bit.

Living next door to *Doddy* Sam

Hello, I'm Daniel's big brother Michael. I'm 13 years old, and I also watch what *Doddy*'s doing. I'm in eighth grade. I help my dad do the farming, and when my chores are done and I get the time, I work in *Doddy*'s shop. I make birdhouses, paint horseshoes, and make songbook stands. *Doddy* lets me use his shop tools, if I put them away again. IF I don't forget. Sometimes I've worked on my pigeon pen and let the tools lie when I've finished. *Doddy* goes, "Grrr, grrr!"

Once I used his cordless drill in the barn and left it lie. *Doddy* couldn't find it for many moons. "Grrr, grr!" When *Doddy* gets busy, I sometimes help in his shop, making sheds and putting on shingles or siding. *Doddy* keeps on teaching me how to do woodworking and painting.

Doddy makes sheds of all kinds and sizes. One time a shed was too wide to go out the door, so *Doddy* had to take away part of the shop wall. Slowly he rolled the shed through the wider opening, and then loaded it on a truck so it could be hauled to the customer. Every now and then *Doddy* makes shed kits, which are put together at the job site. Early in the morning the truck comes and the wall sections are loaded. Then they load the tools, *Doddy* and the boys crawl into the truck, and off they go. At times I also go along and help.

Sometimes *Doddy* gets company from anywhere in the United States or Canada, and often from Germany or Switzerland. In the summertime they sit in the yard, and I get to talk to the visitors. One time Hans Haslibacher the 11th from Switzerland came, along with Amos Hoover, the Mennonite historian, and other people. They sang several songs out in the yard. I liked hearing Hans speak his native High German.

Back in 1995 to 2000, *Doddy* was on the state Amish school board, and he often went away. He said he gave over 500 hours a year to those meetings. Then Uncle Ike and Uncle Amos did a lot of the shop work.

Doddy, the tease

Hello, I'm Katie. I'm 12 years old and in seventh grade. I also see what *Doddy* does around here. Often I help *Dat* do the morning milking. We use old newspapers to wipe the cows' udders. In these newspapers are crossword puzzles. In my spare time during chores, I do the puzzles. *Doddy* calls me "Crossword Kate," which I don't like.

We have an air motor on our washing machine. When I'm doing the laundry, *Doddy* sometimes pinches the air line, which stops the washing machine motor. I frantically try to get the machine going, thinking there's a mechanical problem, but when I look out the window, I see *Doddy* walking away giggling!

Learning for life

Hello, I'm Samuel. I'm in fifth grade. I also help my dad farm, and I often see what *Doddy* is doing. Just lately, *Doddy*'s skid loader got damaged, and so he needs to fix it. Michael and I want to help. *Doddy* says we may if we don't lose any parts.

I just love to ride our horses and zip past the shop. Sometimes I throw a ball—or in the winter, a snowball—at *Doddy*. He hollers, "Now Samuel!"

We have two Jersey cows that I like to lead around. We take them out to the hayfield every day, then bring them in at milking time. I lead them into the barn at the same time, one in each hand. Sometimes they want to go in different directions, and I can't get them headed into the barn. *Doddy* says, "It's hard to say who is leading who!"

Back about 1985, *Doddy* made a machine to shell peas. In 1999, my dad took over the pea-shelling business. Now we children operate the pea sheller during pea season. This year, during the first week in June, *Doddy* and I made a new pea sheller. What fun cutting and welding steel tubing, fitting belts, and making parts out of plastic sheets. Finally it was ready, just as a woman came with peas to shell.

My brother Michael also decorates horseshoes to sell, and my sisters Katie and Naomi stamp cards and sell them. Stop in and buy some!

You can see there's never a dull moment around here!

In the past, the causes of many barn fires were often not determined. Reluctant to press charges if arson has been proven, the Amish tend instead to focus on rebuilding the fallen structure and continuing their farming, rather than seeking investigations and retribution. At the center of successful barnraisings are a willing and experienced community of volunteer carpenters and helpers, and a knowledgeable lead carpenter. Good food, supplied by good cooks and many helpers who also often donate food, are instrumental to the positive atmosphere and efficiency of the project.

CHAPTER SIXTEEN

Barn Fires Span a 10-Year Period

A barn fire is a devastating experience for a farmer, both materially and emotionally. In the space of half an hour, all of a year's crops, a major building, and often animals go up in smoke. The loss is traumatic during the summer, but in the cold of winter it becomes a nightmare. Where can one feed and milk the cows? How can one handle the milk? Where can one find shelter for the young stock?

In this strong agricultural community, for the past 250 years, farmers have always helped each other rebuild, and when the barn was ready, they have shared their own hay, straw, and food for the livestock.

In our Paradise, Pennsylvania, area there have been many barn fires over the years, but there were two periods when the numbers were excessive: during 1963-64 and 1973-74. How the community responded to these losses may be worthy of note for others who may find themselves in similar circumstances.

In November of 1963, just a week prior to the assassination of President Kennedy, Earl Jones' barn along Leacock Road was completely destroyed by fire. The fire companies responded and promptly helped the Jones family get all the animals out of the burning barn.

The next morning, neighbors came from near and far and helped clear away the debris. Carpenter Christ Beiler was asked to oversee rebuilding the barn. Within three weeks, the new barn was practically completed. Because it was winter and Christ wanted to get the barn built quickly, a large crane was used to set the frames and purlins. I was at the raising on that cold day in December, helping to set the rafters and spike the peaks. By December 22, thanks to a lot of donated labor, the Jones family had a new barn. Soon milk checks would start coming again.

Since the Jones family didn't have room to set up a big table to feed the workers, the Gordonville Fire Company auxiliary members prepared meals and served them at the fire hall.

Another incident in the Paradise area happened one month later. On December 22, 1963, a small fire broke out in the upstairs of the barn on the Sylvan Stoltzfus farm, located along the Lincoln Highway. Two burning hay bales fell into the stable area as the Stoltzfus boys were starting the evening milking. Quick work by the family and the Paradise and Gordonville Fire companies saved the barn. Only minor damage was done.

One month later, in January 1964, a barn along Old Leacock Road, owned by Jake (Teddy) Esh, burned. Firemen had the fire under control by daybreak. Throughout the night, women and girls served coffee and sandwiches to the firemen. The next day, help poured in from the neighborhood, as everyone joined in the cleanup work.

Barnraising in bad weather

Carpenter Jake Flaud was asked to build the new barn, an arduous task in good weather, but in the middle of winter, quite a chore. In the cleanup, it was discovered that some new footers were needed. Blocks were laid. Truckloads of lumber were ordered. And each day, 50 to 75 men helped to cut the timbers, make mortise holes, and carry lumber. As usual, lots of food was donated. Many women prepared the meals. Folding church benches were set up to form tables.

On the day of the barnraising, all of the frames were put up and the rafters were set. The next day was cold and damp. By the middle of the day it began to rain. I was helping put on the tin roof; much of the tin was nailed on during the rain. And in about 10 days, the Esh family had a new barn.

It takes about 5,000 to 6,000 hours to build an average-sized Lancaster County barn. About 90% of this labor is donated.

In 1973, another series of barn fires broke out in the Paradise area. On February 5, 1973, again on the Earl Jones farm, the upper part of the barn was destroyed. Late evening cleanup was promptly done by the neighbors. Lydia Scott, who owned the farm, decided not to rebuild. As a result, the cow stable was made usable, and Earl continued farming.

In March of 1973, at about one in the morning, the large, 10-year-old barn on the Mose Stoltzfus farm on Irishtown Road was destroyed by fire. In an almost miraculous fashion, the immediate community responded. Men and boys came with teams of horses and mules, with wagons, and with bulldozers to clean up. The Amish fire insurance man was soon on the scene. A three-man appraisal team determined the value of the loss. And within several days, the appraised amount was paid to the farmer.

Cooperation from the saw mills

Soon the block walls were repaired. Local saw mills keep a good supply of barn timber on hand. So carpenter Christ Beiler moved in with his large crew, lumber began arriving, and about 125 men helped each day to clean up and prepare the foundation.

About eight days later, the materials were ready to set up the barn. On raising day, about 350 men and boys helped, and the barn was soon under roof. After several more days of cleaning up and adding finishing touches, the barn was complete. Moses could begin milking his cattle in the new barn. Loads of donated hay, straw, and corn fodder began arriving. Soon the family had a good supply of food for the animals in the new barn.

Thirty women helped to prepare and serve food to these workers.

While the Amish community was busy helping the Mose Stoltzfus family rebuild their barn, on March 10, 1973, the Saturday night after the Gordonville Mud Sale, about two and a half miles south, the large seven-bay barn on the Joe Lapp farm went up in flames. The upper part of the barn was destroyed, but the stables were partially saved.

Early Monday morning, about 100 men and boys started the cleanup operation. Carpenter Christ Beiler was soon on the scene. Other jobs had to wait while the local saw mills worked overtime to cut lumber for the new barn. By Wednesday, the cleanup and the necessary masonry work were done. Lumber trucks began rolling in, and carpenter Christ, whistling as he went from station to station, kept 80 men busy making mortise and tenon joints, and cutting girders, joists, and rafters.

In about eight days, the preparation was complete and the word was sent out. Early the next morning, about 350 men and boys assembled on the barn floor. The framework went up like magic.

The normal expectation is to have the frames up by 10:00 in the morning, the purlins and rafters by noon, and the lath and roofing by dark. It was a mild March day, and the work went well. Carpenter Christ said this was one of the largest barns he had built.

One might think that farmers aren't very busy in March. Quite the contrary. Plowing, hauling manure, and repair jobs all waited until their neighbor's barn was rebuilt.

Then in June of 1973, at about midnight, the barn on the David Stoltzfus farm burned. Because it was summer, the cattle were in the fields, and the family was able to rescue the remaining livestock—horses, heifers, and the bull. Most of the barn was destroyed, but the stable area was saved. Neighbors came by, and soon the dirty cleanup was done.

Resourceful women

Once again, carpenter Christ Beiler was asked to put up the barn. He set aside his previously scheduled jobs, and he and his crew of six men started at 6:30 each morning. He could be heard whistling as he walked barefooted around the site, carrying his 16" × 24" steel square to measure and mark. His crew, and from 40 to 60 volunteers, cut, chiseled, and drilled mortise holes. Even during the busy planting season, farmers came to help. Women set out the 9:00 a.m. coffee and cookie break, then made and served a full-course dinner at 11:30. At 3:00 in the afternoon, they offered a substantial snack with more coffee, cookies, sandwiches, and apples. Many farmers helped until 4:00, and then rushed home to do their milking without starving, until their evening meal around 7:30.

Since Dave B. Stoltzfus was an active member of the Gordonville Fire Company, many of the firemen came to help on the day of the raising. I was there the next day to help with finishing touches. By the end of the raising day, however, the barn was nearly complete.

Five months later, on November 29, 1973, in West Gordonville, Andrew Kinsinger's 110-year-old barn went up in smoke in the early evening. The barn, its contents, and several pigs burned. Cleanup started the next day. Andrew decided not to build on the same spot, but to put up the new barn about 1,600 feet west of the burned-out one. A small building located at that spot was removed. Carpenter Christ Beiler started the building of the new barn. Volunteers came by, footers were dug, concrete was poured, and blocks laid. Andrew had many friends because of his printing business and work with Amish schools. Many of them came to help. The barn went up rapidly, and despite bad weather, the roof of the new barn was in place about 10 days after the fire.

The Kinsingers were hog farmers, and so their barn could be much smaller than a typical dairy barn. Only hog pens, box stalls, and a forebay on the first floor were needed. In about two and a half weeks, the barn was complete. The following spring, Andy hired a bulldozer and several dump trucks to haul the barn hill from the site of the burned barn to the new one. The last traces of the Kauffman barn, which Sam Kauffman built for his son John in the 1860s, had disappeared.

When an historic barn burns

The fires continued. Two months later, in February of 1974, the 200-year-old barn on widow Mary Stoltzfus' farm went up in flames about 5:00 in the morning. This barn had been built by Rev. John Woodhull in 1769. Its stone walls survived, but the upper barn was destroyed. The floor planking had to be replaced, but the 50'-long original joists could be reused.

It took lots of work to pull down the stone walls. The 200-year-old mortar mixed with clay, lime, and pig's hair was still hard.

Christ Beiler was asked to make the new barn. Soon scores of volunteers were on the scene and clearing debris. As soon as the lumber arrived, Christ and his crew marked the beams, posts, and braces. Then chain saws began roaring, boring machines were putt-putting, and hammers were put to work hitting steel chisels.

I helped on the day before the raising. Carpenter Christ was a man of few words. As he gave his orders, he also instructed several neighbor volunteers at the same time. He showed us how to line up floor joists by using a transit level and shims of varying sizes and thicknesses. There was a lot of trial and error and checking of many sight lines until the top side of the 200-year-old, 50'-long logs of oak and walnut were on one plane. Planking was temporarily laid down, and the barn went up the next day.

Often outsiders ask, "How do so many men know what's to be done?" Since most farmers are practical and do most of their own repair work, barn parts and barn construction are as common as bread and butter to them. Hammers fit their hands like gloves. Most men attend six or eight barnraisings a year, so the skills are not forgotten. A good carpenter boss like Christ Beiler can spot farmers with major building skills to be group leaders for a segment of the work. He also knows that about 15% of the men assembled are older men who are just watching, and that there are always a bunch of visitors. With his people skills, it seems as if the barn goes up by itself.

Women from these families always prepare the meals and snacks, and they may work on a quilt together if there's time when they're not serving food.

The Stoltzfus barn went up in about nine days. The widow, and her son, Elam, who had just been married three months before, could now put their cows in the new barn.

Amish young people are strongly encouraged by their families and church to socialize. They need the change to balance a long week of work. They hope to marry, and social events within their faith community are where they are likely to find their spouses.

Rumspringa *is understood by parents and the church to be a time when young people grow to be responsible for their own behavior and, it is strongly hoped, choose to become members of the Amish church. They are baptized upon their confession of faith, usually in their late teens. Sometimes young people experiment with boundaries during* **Rumspringa,** *causing much concern for their parents and church leaders. An ongoing question is how much control should families and the church attempt?*

CHAPTER SEVENTEEN

A Brief History of Supervised Youth Groups in Lancaster County

In 1999, two Lancaster bishops became concerned about Amish youth group activities. They attended the first meeting of parents who were discussing whether these get-togethers should have parental supervision. The bishops supported this move.

Now it seems that if the parents and leaders had known then the amount of work involved and the prayers that would be needed, they probably would have felt faint.

But first a little history about Amish youth groups. Ever since Jakob Ammann took action that led to the Amish movement beginning in 1693, there have been youth groups and a system for finding marriage partners within the Amish community. Even from the 1750s to the 1770s, we know of youth groups in the first Amish settlement in America in Berks County, Pennsylvania, getting out of hand. And we recall hearing that youth became unruly in Civil War times, some even enlisting in the Union Army.

Tensions

There has been much concern through the years about reforming youth groups in Lancaster County. This was a seedbed for the Conestoga and Millwood meetinghouse split in the 1870s. About 40 percent of the Lancaster Amish left the church in this split. For nearly 30 years, the Old Order young people didn't drive past the meetinghouses to avoid being heckled and having things thrown at their passing buggies. Not everything was under control. Also, in some western states, several church splits were fostered by leaders who said they desired more spirituality for the youth. But each split was soon followed by more liberal practices, and soon the Amish way of life or name wasn't visible.

In 1966, a New Order split took place in Lancaster. Many who left said they wanted a deeper spirituality in their youth groups. However, in less than 10 years, many youth in the New Order group chose not to stay, and divisions continued until there were six or more New Order factions.

In the early to mid-1900s, there was a serious problem in the Lancaster County village of Intercourse. Young people first gathered at the Cross Keys hotel during the years 1920 to 1940. Then at Hess Mill from the 1940s to the 1960s. Then at the frozen custard stand through 1970. Then at the Pensupreme store up to 1980. Young people would get together there on Saturday and Sunday nights to find out what was happening, and then often became quite unruly, until the police were sometimes called. Many bishops and parents were concerned, but little was done to correct the situation.

In the 1980s, as chairman of the Amish National Steering Committee, Andrew Kinsinger wrote a letter of concern for the media, to be read in every Lancaster Amish church district. This public voicing of the problem helped to a degree, but, sad to say, the letter wasn't approved by many Lancaster bishops. From roughly 1950 to 1990, 15 percent of the Lancaster Amish youth weren't really under control.

A pivotal moment

In 1998, two Amish boys were arrested and convicted of hardcore drug dealing. This led to much undesirable publicity, as national and international reporters covered every detail possible about the court trials. This finally aroused nearly all Lancaster Amish parents. Late in the summer of 1998, an Upper Pequea district family wrote a letter about the dangers of drug use, which was read at the close of many Amish church services, but not all. Again, some bishops voiced their disapproval.

In late 1998, there were many meetings of concerned parents and ministers. Soon two young prominent Lancaster bishops attended the meetings to offer support and assist in writing guidelines for newly forming youth groups. These would be *supervised* youth groups which were starting from scratch, with the backing and approval of parents and youth alike.

By January 10, 1999, guidelines were approved and printed for a new youth group called the Eagles. They had their first singing under the auspices and with the blessing of an Upper Millcreek bishop.

Many parents soon noted that the Eagle youth didn't support as conservative a dress style as they thought was necessary. This led to separate meetings, resulting in the Hummingbird group forming. This group developed their own guidelines, including more conservative dress standards. Their first Sunday singing was held September 5, 1999, with the support of a Lower Pequea district bishop.

As the new century began, there was a feeling of thankfulness and praise that now there were better choices for youth who desired proper *Rumspringa* and courtship. Several main changes were made to improve conditions for youth activities:

- There would be no Saturday evening gatherings.
- Sunday gatherings for supper and evening singing would take place at the same home. This eliminated large groups of buggies on the road at one time.
- Singings would start at 7:00 p.m. using the *Ausbund* hymnal for one hour, followed by singing from the *Unpartheyisches Gesangbuch* for one hour.
- A light snack would be served, with no outside activities.
- Everyone must leave by 10:00 p.m.

The Lancaster senior bishop soon expressed his approval, saying he was so thankful that efforts were made to get the youth home at an earlier hour.

However, some parents still wished for a more conservative dress code and preferred that their children not use closed carriages. By early 2002, meetings were held, and with the support of a Millcreek bishop and several Groffdale ministers, a third new group was formed who would use open buggies. With much prayer and the encouragement of about 15 sets of concerned parents, the group called Parakeets started. Their first singings were in the spring of 2002.

All three of the new groups used the same basic guidelines. Each had a five-man advisory board consisting of bishops and ministers who would serve five-year terms. A three-man caretaker board, chosen from among the parents, also served three-or five-year terms. By 2003, approximately 600 Lancaster County

Amish youth were in supervised groups.

The future for supervised groups looked bright. Many parents from all over Lancaster County hoped to extend supervision to existing groups.

Continuing change

But in early 2005, there were growing pains. Soon the Hummingbirds grew so large that it was necessary to divide the group. This was done by a vote, and a geographical line was agreed upon, so now there were two singings. Those going steady with a girlfriend or boyfriend in the other group could choose which group to attend. Soon both groups were quite large. Then another line was made, and now there were four geographical areas. Four advisory boards and four caretaker boards were installed, one for each area.

At the same time, the Eagle group was growing rapidly, so it was necessary to form two geographical areas for it. Again, a line was agreed on, and two singings began. Within several years, both groups became too large, so again a line was agreed on, and then there were four suppers and singings scheduled.

Another blessing of the supervised groups was the development of a complete list of the boys and girls who belonged, including their addresses, and in some cases phone numbers. And there was a written schedule of the planned singings, sometimes six or eight weeks in advance. This eliminated much guesswork about where the next gathering would be held, and those who didn't have transportation could plan to travel with those who had room.

Another great blessing was the twice-a-year meetings in each supervised group. Both the parents and youth attended these three-hour meetings. And the 15-year-olds who would be joining these specific youth groups were invited. At the meeting, the guidelines were read and explained. If there were questions, they were addressed.

If someone had broken rules, a punishment was decided. The caretaker board would visit the wrongdoers and inform the young person what was required to make amends. Usually a first offense punishment was a formal apology to the caretakers. For second or third offenses, the person stayed home for several Sundays. This was the most effective consequence and wasn't needed often. If there were too many repeat offenses, the next step was to expel the wrongdoers. These twice-a-year meetings became very important to maintaining a working supervised youth group.

Was the supervised youth group movement the answer to all youth problems? Did the parents always agree? Of course not, although the cooperation was remarkable at times. By the spring of 2006, as many groups needed to divide again, disagreements became apparent. In the more liberal groups, cell phones and various electronic devices were creeping in. Although the rules forbade overnight gatherings in most supervised groups, such gatherings sometimes took place. Enforcing the dress code was also a problem, a cause of stress among parents. In 2008, one group appointed a special committee to assist in punishing the offenders. But there was disagreement among the committee about what to do, so little was accomplished.

Considering the future

What is the likely future for Lancaster County supervised youth groups? There have been many blessings and some disgraces. Recently, some groups have become too large again, and disagreements developed about how to divide the groups. In two or three cases, instead of agreeing to divide the too-large groups, a set of parents and youth formed a new group. While on the surface, harmony appeared to be restored, the problem situation was not resolved. There seems to be movement toward relaxing our discipline, at least in some places. For example, even in the group who preferred open buggies, more closed carriages are being used. Some parents paid for them.

It appears that to form a successful supervised youth group:

Parents must be in harmony, working and praying together.

The bishop must support a supervised group.

Start from scratch, with both the parents and youth willing to make a fresh start.

Be aware that the youth will make good choices and bad choices. Whatever happens, everyone involved should be willing to communicate and work together.

After nearly 20 years of supervised youth groups, we can see many blessings. Two examples: Young women from supervised groups make better schoolteachers. And young men from supervised groups who are ordained make better church leaders. The time, effort, and prayers put into starting and maintaining supervised youth groups has been a good investment for our future Old Order Amish churches.

CHAPTER EIGHTEEN

A Year on an Amish Farm

Farming is 24-7, year-round labor. But a farm is a good place to raise a family. We were blessed to be able to buy 41 acres of land in 1974, and then make a set of buildings over the next several years. After that, we waded into the rigors of milking cows, floating interest rates, milk inspectors, and rising taxes.

Since we had bought bare land in 1974 and made new buildings from 1976 to 1979, we lived on a shoestring budget. We had very little money for new equipment, so in the winter, we went to farm sales to work on our wish list and to see what we could afford. Maybe we could get something at a giveaway price. It might at least have parts that we could use.

In the wintertime, farmers should do three things: read the Bible, haul manure, and love their wives, not necessarily in that order. It's a good feeling to have all the manure spread in the fields that you want to plow, come spring. Other winter jobs are to grease and repair the harnesses and farm equipment, and catch up on honey-dos for your wife. It's a good time, too, to go to feed company meetings and farm sales, and to help some neighbor or friend work on his building project. And clip the mules and horses so they feel like working.

Back in 1978 when I worked for a Lancaster home construction company and we were building a new house in Maryland, we drove past a forsaken-looking farm every day. I noticed many old horse-drawn implements sitting outside, looking like they could have heard Civil War cannons. I stopped one day and met the farm owner, an elderly woman. She had never met any Amish and was delighted to know that someone would want her almost worn-out, horse-drawn pieces. I was able to make a deal with her and trucked home five pieces that gave me years of service.

Spring excitement

When the fields are ready and the weather is nice, the spring rush starts. It's the beginning of an ag marathon of sorts—Farmers, Start Your Enzymes. Nothing gets a farmer's and mule's or horse's adrenalin pumping faster than a fine spring morning when there's fieldwork to do. Your wife can't understand why you've gulped your breakfast down in several bites, or why you have no time to play with the baby. Instead, you race to the barn, slap on the harnesses, hitch up the team, and plow an acre before 9:00 a.m.

Neighbors race to be the first one plowing, or the first to mow rye or triticale (a spring legume), or the first to plant corn. It's the talk at Sunday church. "Did you see Jake is cutting alfalfa?" Skeptics shake their heads: "It can't be mature yet."

Women are in the race also. "Did you hear Katie is housecleaning already?" "Really? I didn't start yet." And it's always fun to have a long washline filled with flapping laundry before any of the neighbors. But if any woman is laid up due to having a baby or sickness, rest assured, all the women in the neighborhood will lay their work aside to help the one in need.

The same is true of the men. If any farmer is sick or has a bad back or broken leg, someone will promptly plan a work day. And early the next morning, six or eight teams will be in the ailing farmer's fields, hauling manure, plowing or planting corn, or making hay.

Come June, the race is still in high gear. Corn-planting follows the first cutting of hay; the second cutting of alfalfa happens alongside planting and picking produce. If there's an Amish holiday, both mules and farmers are glad for a day of rest. But if there's a barn fire or a death in the neighborhood, the teams stop their own work, and all available neighbors go to offer assistance.

In the old days, when all the farmers had wheat, there were six to eight days of threshing in early July. We never grew wheat because by the mid1970s, wheat prices weren't profitable. Besides, alfalfa contains much more protein than wheat. But our boys and I would help *Dat* and cousin Sam thresh, because threshing was still instilled in our genes, and it was a good experience for our boys.

In August, there are weeds to hoe and the third cutting of alfalfa to make. The tobacco harvest will soon start. (We never raised tobacco, but we helped *Dat*.) In late August we open the cornfields, mainly because our silos are almost empty.

Fun breaks

Back in the 1950s when I was still at home, in mid-July *Dat* would say, "Now, children let's work real fast and hoe all the weeds in the tobacco and cornfields. Then we'll take a day off and go to the New Holland Horse Sale.

Suddenly our energy and hoes moved at a rate approaching the speed of light. With *Dat* in the lead, five or six of us headed to the fields. Woe to any weeds that were within range of our hoes. Some cornstalks and tobacco also fell victim.

Then early on a Monday morning, *Dat* would hitch our driving horse, Bobby, to the spring wagon. The four or five oldest children piled on, and we traveled the eight-mile, one-hour trip to New Holland. It was quite an experience to see the horses and mules being sold. Cigar-chomping ring man John Gingerich expounded on the virtues of the animal on the block. At times he pried open the horse's mouth and hollered, "Five-year-old. Is the owner here?"

When the auctioneer's chant began to lose its rapture, I'd ask *Dat* if I could tour the New Holland Baler plant on Franklin Street, just a short walk away. At that time, anyone could walk in and watch the Super 77 balers being put together. *Dat* and Uncle Sylvan had just purchased their first brand new New Holland Super 77 baler, and it was a large part of my cousins', and my landscape.

All too soon it was time to head home and back to the routine of farm work. For weeks, my cousins and I played horse sale, impersonating the ring man and the auctioneer. Cousin John always played ring man John Gingerich, hollering, "Is the owner here?" Then he pried open our mouths and announced, "Four-year-old well broke." At that time in our little minds, the world only went to New Holland and as far south as our church districts.

Another reward trip *Dat* and *Mam* would promise us was to go to the Rough and Tumble Threshermen's Reunion held in Kinzers in early August. This was also an hour-long trip in the spring wagon. Four or five of us would go along and spend the day watching dozens of steam engines and threshing machines in operation. At noon, all the steam whistles would blow, and we'd sit in a picnic area and eat our packed lunches. Sometimes *Dat* would buy us ice cream cones, a rare treat. It wasn't that we loved seeing all the old equipment, because we had an old tractor and threshing machine which we actually used once a year. But our cousins would be there the same day we were. And in those days, anyone could pretend to drive the tractors. That was great sport, and we often did it till the management chased us off.

Working together

We started farming ourselves in 1979. Early September of 1978 was our first silo-filling season. We worked together with my cousin Sam and *Dat*. Silo-filling is one of the most labor-intensive operations in the fall harvest. With three wagons hauling, along with one man and often a young woman driving the wagon beside the binder, it took about two days to fill a 12′ × 60′ silo, and then another day to refill it because the silage settled. Since we each had two silos, we were filling silo for some two weeks.

Our next job was to sow the rye cover crop, followed by picking corn. *Dat* and I worked together, picking corn on our two farms. If the weather was nice and the fields were dry, we could finish in two weeks. Then the last job before winter was to chop and harvest the corn fodder and haul it in. By then it was wedding season, and soon another year was past.

In early January, it was time to go over the books and see where all the income went, if there was any. Mostly it all was outcome in those early years, because we were in the clutches of Farm Credit and floating interest rates which were 7% in 1977—lower than the banks' 8%. But because it was a *floating* rate—or more correctly, a *zooming* rate—it was soon 9%, then 11%, and eventually 12%. It was an unreal world. Our monthly payments were some $900.00, and a large part of it was interest. We were at the point of despair, and then a kindhearted neighbor offered to take over our mortgage at the fixed rate of 8%. It was a lifesaver for our family and farm.

Was there a blessing in having paid all that interest? Of course. Think of all the money that was available to folks who were taking out loans at Farm Credit because of all the interest money we paid in over the years.

Side businesses

When the boys completed school, we started a wood-working business, which turned out to be a good venture. It gave the boys and me valuable life experience. We also started to raise horseradish for a company in Baltimore.

We didn't have facilities to raise tobacco, and I detested working with tobacco, although we did help *Dat* harvest his crop. Also, in the early '80s, tobacco profits took a nose dive. So we planted two acres of horseradish, harvested it in early November, and trucked it to Baltimore. It was profitable, but it was nothing glamorous. My wife was taught to waste nothing, and she noticed that the horseradish digger had missed some roots in the field. So she dug them up, cranked them through a hand-grinder, and sold the product to folks in Gordonville. I was a bit skeptical at first, but it soon turned into a profitable venture. Today, 34 years, later it is good retirement work.

CHAPTER NINETEEN

The Responsibility of Being Amish Parents

A little background

I am the oldest in a large family of 14, with nine sisters and four brothers. Our parents were Gideon and Mary Stoltzfus. We grew up on a 75-acre dairy and poultry farm in Leacock Township, just west of the village of Gordonville.

Since I had nine sisters, when I turned 16 and got my own horse and buggy, it seemed I was often trucking one or more of them here and there. That didn't make me very excited about stepping into the dating world. But I had different thoughts when I discovered that my fourth sister had a very interesting and good-looking girlfriend. I quickly changed my attitude about females, and we began dating when she was 17. We got married on October 31, 1967, when she was 20 and I was 24.

Choosing a spouse

Some of our people encourage young men to ask these four questions when choosing whom to marry:

- Does she know the Bible?
- Does she know how to plant a garden, and then harvest, can, and freeze the garden goodies?
- Does she know how to harness a horse, hitch it to a carriage, and go visiting or shopping?
- Does she enjoy caring for her little nieces and nephews or her younger siblings?

They believe that if a woman does all four well, she will make a good wife.

I didn't worry about such details. I married for love! I want to thank God for a good wife.

As was typical of Amish weddings in the late '60s, we were married in my wife's 40-year-old frame farm house on a nice fall day. About 350 guests were invited. Our honeymoon consisted of visiting my 14 aunts and uncles and Katie's 13 aunts and uncles, plus dozens of cousins, neighbors, and friends on weekends all winter long. We received wedding presents at each visit.

In March of 1968, we moved into a little two-story brick house. Compared to today's plain-folk lifestyle, we lived in medieval times. A big coal stove provided our heat. The bathroom consisted of a commode and a washbowl. To bathe, you put hot water in a basin, put your dirty clothes on a pile on the floor, sat on them Indian-style, and gave yourself a sponge bath. In the summer-time, we got out a big galvanized tub, set it in the kettle house, heated water in the iron kettle, and poured it into the tub. Oh, that was bathing bliss. But those were happy times for us. I was able to keep my conscientious objector status because I worked on my brother-in-law's farm (for 75 cents an hour).

First baby shock

As is often the case, Amish newlyweds have a baby in their first year of marriage, and we were no different. Our first son was born in August of 1968, in the hospital. At that time, midwives didn't deliver a first-born baby at home.

Suddenly we were in the whirlwind of changing diapers and nursing, with a baby who slept in the daytime and was awake at night, and a mother who was always tired.

We became quickly aware that Amish babies are just like all babies—they don't come with instructions. The maid who came to assist with all the housework in those first weeks helped to get the baby on a schedule. And thanks to Dr. Kaiser and her well-thought-out instructions, we soon had a happy baby.

When he was six weeks old, we took him along to church. This is quite a ritual for first-time Amish parents, including packing the baby basket with plenty of diapers (Pampers weren't in our budget) and the father handing the baby in to the mother once she was in the carriage. My mother-in-law insisted that Katie not climb in while holding the baby for safety reasons. Then we drove to wherever the worship service was being held, no matter the distance.

Since our services often last three hours, a mother usually has to take the baby upstairs to nurse and for a nap. After the fellowship meal, the family heads home. The mother may be able to relax to a degree, as friends and relatives often come visiting Sunday afternoons to see the newborn and bring a baby gift.

Our babies were born with a liver deficiency and would soon turn yellow, so they had to go to the hospital and be put under a special light for several days. Fortunately, they all responded well to that.

One and a half years after our first child, we were blessed with another son. Now we had two little guys to dress in the morning, to change their diapers whenever needed, and to make sure they were fed well. Then there was potty-training, teaching them simple German child prayers at first, and then the Lord's Prayer in German. As they neared school age, we taught them basic English, so that by the time they went to school, they could understand the language well enough to learn to read the first-grade-level books.

In December of 1971, our healthy first daughter was born. The next day we had to take her to the hospital, but after four days there, she came home again. Our hospital bill was $500.00, and my Christmas bonus that year was $500.00, so the bill was covered.

It takes a church district. . .

An old saying tells us that it takes a village to raise a child. In our plain-folks world, we note that it takes a church district to raise a family. Fortunately, there is always a grandma who knows how to give treatments to a colicky baby. And there are many young girls who delight in babysitting if a mother has a small baby and her older children need attention. Since I worked for a contractor in Lancaster and was away 11 hours a day, we had a part-time maid to help with the housework.

In 1974, another healthy daughter joined our family. That same year, our oldest son stepped into school life, starting first grade in the nearby one-room Amish school. I took that first day off from work and went with him to school. That began a new chapter in our lives, helping with lessons, packing lunches, and keeping tabs on report cards. Also in 1974, we bought a 40-acre farm. By 1975, we were in the busy world of building a house and shop.

Parents and church together

As soon as the children were old enough to take part, we developed a special family prayer time in the evenings. And on Sunday evenings we sang together.

In 1975, our oldest son turned nine and started going in with the boys at worship services (see pages 9-13). We had a practice in our family that went back several previous generations.

As boys and girls approached their ninth birthday, they needed to memorize the "Lobelied." This 28-line, four-verse German hymn is in the *Ausbund*, our church hymnal. Our children all did it.

In January of 1976, we moved into our new house. By then, the oldest children could help their mother wash lots of dishes and do some of the laundry.

In 1978 we built a dairy barn, and in 1979 we were milking cows. Now the children could help with the barn chores, and the boys soon learned to drive the team to do fieldwork.

We kept learning as parents, too, realizing that all children are different. Our oldest was more mechanically minded and loved to work with tools. Our second loved to work with animals— from feeding the calves to driving the team in the fields.

In January of 1977, we were blessed with another healthy daughter. Like our earlier babies, she turned a bit yellow on the second day, and in the middle of a January blizzard, I took this little one to the hospital in an ambulance (see pages 76-80). Several days later, thankfully, she was doing well.

In June of 1979, another healthy son joined our family. As per the midwife's instructions, we kept the baby in the sun as much as possible so he didn't need a hospital stay.

In 1981, another daughter joined us, and we surmised our family was complete. Then in 1987, another son came along—a big fellow who seemed to have a jumpstart on life. And in 1990, we had another son. He was a bit frail and didn't grow well at first, but with our oldest daughter's help and a special formula, he soon outgrew his siblings. Now our family was complete.

Some horse and buggy folks say that the best family time is when everyone fits into one carriage when the whole family goes away together.

When our children were fairly young, we purchased a set of Bible storybooks, and when they were old enough to understand, we gave each of them a German and an English New Testament. We also subscribed to the monthly magazines, *Family Life* and *Young Companion*, produced by the Amish Pathway Publishing in Ontario.

As many Amish do, we gave our sons six German books, one each Christmas as they entered their mid-teens, so they had them all before they got married. The books are *The History of the Patriarchs, Lust Gartlein Seelen (Pleasure Garden of Pious Souls)*, the *Unpartheyisches Gesangbuch*, an *Ausbund, Das Gebet* (a prayerbook), and a full-size *Luther Bible* in German.

Stepping out

In 1984 we stepped into another category—*Rumspringa*—when our oldest turned 16. We had given him a harness and items he would need for his team on previous birthdays. But now was the time to buy him a horse and a buggy, battery, and blankets. It's a big concern to find both a *safe* horse *and* one that will go the miles your son wants to travel. We carried the concern—and prayers—that he wouldn't stay out too late and would come home safe. But it was an exciting family time as our oldest developed a circle of friends and we could host the youth group and their hymn sings.

Soon our second son was 16, and we needed to build a buggy shed. Then our oldest daughter turned 16, and we started another chapter when she brought home a boyfriend. Now we all focused on cleaning up the whole place on Saturday afternoons, including getting the parlor ready for company and making a special snack for the boyfriend. It was a delight to see the young folks going away Sunday afternoons and waving good-bye to them.

It seemed our oldest had just started dating, when in 1990, we were attending his wedding—a special day for our family. After the ceremony, the district deacon gave my brain a jolt when he said, "Now you have a Grandparent License." There's an old tale that says your oldest grandchildren should be a bit younger than your youngest children. So it was for us. Our youngest child was seven months old when our oldest son got married, and eventually our youngest son was two years older than our oldest grandson!

CHAPTER TWENTY

How Our Amish Church Districts Are Formed

Ever since hot air balloons began making their aerial visits across Lancaster County Amish country on Sunday mornings, balloon passengers have been mystified about where the buggies are going for church services. Why, these visitors wonder, is one string of buggies going to one place, and often close by, another string of buggies is converging at another place?

Each Amish church district is a geographical area defined either by roads, railroads, creeks, or power lines—or sometimes just by a line on a map without an easy explanation for its location. Long ago in 1843, the first two districts were designated by a little stream which crossed Lancaster County. Then, as more families moved into both the north and south districts, another line was drawn to create new districts.

When is it time?

The process is always the same. When there are 40 or more families, and not enough upstairs rooms in the homes hosting worship services to hold all the sleeping babies, it's time to form a new district. Or when not everyone can hear the preacher, then it's time to divide the district.

A special council is called from among the members, and all of them must agree on the line the ministers have proposed. When that happens, the ministry announces that the district is now divided.

There are serious consequences to forming a new district. Four new ministers are needed, which especially affects the younger married members. These new leaders will likely be drawn from among them. It takes a new bench wagon, set of benches, and folding chairs. A new set of *Ausbunds* (German hymnals) are needed, and a new set of church dishes must be bought to put in the wagon. Generally, it costs $300.00 to $400.00 per family to establish a new church district. (We understand that it can cost the horse-and-buggy Mennonites a thousand dollars or more per family to maintain their meetinghouses.) We strive to keep our more than 300-year-old tradition, started in 1693 by Jacob Ammann, of having our services in our homes.

Today there are over 200 church districts in the Lancaster County Amish settlement, with more than 20,000 members. Let us give God the glory and be thankful for his many blessings.

CHAPTER TWENTY-ONE

An 11-Hour Getaway in Upper Pequea

About 9:30 in the morning, a robber entered the Northwest Savings Bank along West Orange St. in Lancaster. After ordering everyone to lie down, he emptied the cash drawers and took off. First he dashed to a nearby parking garage and changed clothes, which were stored in a suitcase he was carrying. His next move was to hail a taxi, ordering the cabbie to take him to Philadelphia, 80 miles away.

It's an eight-mile jaunt east on Route 30 to Ronks, through heavy traffic and nine traffic lights, a 20-minute trip. It probably seemed longer to the nervous robber and cabbie, especially after a description of the robber came over the radio. No doubt the cabbie glanced in his rear view mirror and thought, Hmm, this looks like the suspected robber! About that time he received orders over his radio to call the office.

The taxi driver swung off Route 30 at the Ronks Road convenience store and stepped over to the pay phone. The robber saw his chance, left his cumbersome suitcase behind, and dashed off through the springtime countryside. He zipped east about 250 yards north of Route 30, behind Millers Smorgasbord, Dieners Restaurant, and Dutch Haven, and then went on through Sam Fishers', Joe Fishers' and Ivan Fishers' fields behind their houses and through their gardens for about a half-mile to Soudersburg Road.

This was probably the first time the suspect had set foot in the Upper Pequea. I'm guessing he wasn't appreciating the beautiful scenery, the green fields with cows peacefully grazing, farmers mowing and raking hay, and women busy in their lawns and gardens. His prime concern now was to get away from the law.

Jogger or robber?

The suspect trotted north on Soudersburg Road to the Ivan and Steven Fisher farm. He headed toward the barnyard, spied Mrs. Steven Fisher in the front yard, and made a quick 180 turn and continued north. About 230 yards further along, he came to Allen Fisher's home, where he headed in the driveway. But after seeing Mrs. Fisher doing yard work, he beat a hasty retreat. Across the road is the home of Steve and Anna Fisher. As the suspect jogged past, Anna waved Hi to him. It's not unusual to see joggers or tourists walking here in the Pequea.

Then the suspect kept trotting north on Soudersburg Road to the home of Sam and Linda Lapp. No one was home there, so he scooted across the lawn to the barn, into the horse stable *fodda gung* (entry), up the narrow steps, and across the main barn to the floor above the corn shed. Here he climbed behind a 20" × 36" × 8'-long triangular shaped hole behind a pile of doors and windows sitting upright against the north gable end.

He'd been on the run for about 11 hours; meanwhile, the State Police headquarters had turned into a war preparation zone. A helicopter was dispatched, and police cruisers headed east with sirens and blinkers going and radios crackling. Law enforcement was looking for the suspect in the Soudersburg area.

Upon hearing the sirens and seeing the police, the two Fisher women held a hasty roadside conference. Might that jogger be the person the police are looking for? They didn't have to wonder long as the police helicopter came flying overhead and police cars cruised north on the Soudersburg Road.

Mrs. Steve Fisher headed for the phone shanty to call her husband about the happenings at home. But before she could finish her call, a cop ordered her to go home and lock her doors. A bank robber was on the loose.

Law enforcement moves in

Even the cows, mules, and chickens knew something was amiss. Like an angry bumblebee, the helicopter circled over the Allen Fishers' house and the Jess Lapps' house, then made a wider circle over to Steven and Ike Fishers' homes. Cows stampeded in the pastures. Mules and horses spooked. Dogs howled as more cop cars came. Flags were put up at Route 30 and Irishtown Rd. Police were in Gordonville and on Route 30.

Back at the State Police headquarters the crime force took over dispatching. More officers, detectives, and plain clothesmen were called in. The suspect had last been seen along North Soudersburg Road near the line between East Lampeter and Leacock townships.

The cab driver was questioned. A man with bloodhounds was called in. The suspect's suitcase was raided, and a pair of shoes from it was sniffed by the bloodhounds. Now the dogs had the scent they needed.

Mrs. Allen Fisher and Mrs. Steve Fisher were questioned. They told the officers they had seen a man jogging north. The hounds picked up the still hot trail as up the road they went, noses to the ground. But as they crossed Sam Lapps' lawn, they seemed to lose the trail.

By now a police command post was set up at Dynamic Masonry's front parking lot. A local TV van cruised about, poking its camera into the Pequea neighborhood. They were shooting pictures of the women in their gardens, animals in the barnyards, and children who were astonished at all the worldly doings.

An effective hiding spot

A white flag roadblock was set up at several entrance roads to the designated area, with police kindly informing motorists of the search. Jess Lapp stopped his mower team behind the suspect's hiding place and inquired about what was happening. Other teams in the neighborhood also got a rest.

By 10:30 that morning, a full day after the robbery, the probe was in full gear. A helicopter buzzed overhead as six cops moved into Sam Lapps' 32' × 40' bank barn. With guns drawn, they peered into the stable, the tobacco and corn shed area, up the narrow steps into the grain bins, and through the hay loft. They looked where Jess's well greased grain binder sat. No doubt the suspect was trembling with fear. The hounds barked as they sniffed through the barn without finding anything. The handler figured they were barking because of Sam's prized white Labradors outside in their pens, who were also barking at all the commotion.

Without a doubt, Lapps' old barn had never seen such a fracas before. It's difficult to explain why the suspect wasn't seen, with the floor having cracks a country-inch wide, and the north gable end boards likewise. The cops put their guns back in their holsters and moved on to Jess Lapps' place. They went through the barn and outbuildings, even looking into the stinky manure spreader. Next they moved to my dad's place and checked out the barn there. Not many stones were left unturned as the cops peered into road culverts and walked through alfalfa fields. Another team went through the Gordonville area house by house, even breaking into one place where no one was home.

Teams in the fields got some rest as the farmers watched the search. Another copter was called in from Maryland with a special infrared detector that could locate a rabbit in an alfalfa patch, but it missed the 180-pound suspect. It was said that the detector worked better at night.

The helicopter made a loud whistling sound, causing the cows to stampede, no doubt causing a drop in milk production. Mules balked and chicken crowded together, probably resulting in fewer eggs.

Jess Lapp went back to mowing hay in the field behind the barn where the suspect was still hiding, while the search went on. They checked Hersheys' Woods; a cop walked through the woods behind our farm. At 5 p.m. the search was called off. Nothing had been found. It seemed the suspect had made a clean getaway. One cop was heard to say, "This was a fun day."

However, sometime during the afternoon, the suspect had crawled out of his uncomfortable hiding spot and made a refuge out of 10 hay bales in the south haymow. Now at least he could stretch out in his little hotel room.

Later in the afternoon, Mrs. Sam Lapp came home. She and her mother worked in the yard right outside the barn. Soon Sam arrived home, went upstairs in the haymow, and saw the bale house. He couldn't remember putting those bales there, but didn't search further because it was supper-time. After eating, the family went away for the evening, with the suspect still holed up in their barn.

On the run again

Sometime after dark, the suspect crawled out of his hole and ran down the Soudersburg Road, almost bumping into Ivan Fisher, who was putting away his brand new corn planter. The suspect kept going toward Route 30, where he turned east. Someone reported a guy running along Route 30, who seemed different than a jogger. Almost instantly, three police cars were on the scene. They drove up to the suspect with their guns drawn and forced him to lie down. Mr. Sheets, the suspect, was handcuffed and hauled off to prison.

So our peace-loving, Upper Pequea Amish church district citizens felt at ease again. Everybody in the Soudersburg area could get a good night's sleep. Sam Lapp put his hay bales back in their proper place. Jess Lapps', Ike Fishers', and Ivan Fishers' cows returned to grazing and providing milk, the chickens went back into egg production, and the horses and mules resumed pulling the hay mowers and bale wagons again. Life in the Upper Pequea was back in its proper peaceful order.

Thanks to the state and county police for conducting the search and providing proper protection while letting the busy farmers continue with their hay-making. And thanks, Mr. Sheets, for staying in hiding, rather than harming our busy, peace-loving farmers and their families.

CHAPTER TWENTY-TWO

Horse Training

Want a college degree in horse training? You don't need to enroll in any university or pay a five-digit tuition if you attend Henry Hershberger's horseman's clinic held at various farms and blacksmith shops in Ohio and Pennsylvania.

We bought a nice standardbred with some Morgan background for our son Elmer last winter. The little gal is easy to hitch and a good traveler, but she spooked nastily at large trucks, dashing off the road. So when blacksmith Jonas Riehl advertised an equine school, I committed myself, part of my checkbook, and this seven-year-old mare to attend.

Early on the morning of May 7, I drove over to blacksmith Jonas Riehl's farm and unhitched the mare. Jonas told me to take off the harness and put the horse in the stall. Henry would come soon.

At 8:30, Henry and his crew pulled in. Henry is of Amish background, and he and his wife speak Pennsylvania Dutch. They unloaded their saddles and gear over lots of horse conversation and coffee-drinking. Fifteen minutes later, Jonas said, "Bring your horse over and put her in the round pen. Let her wander around and get used to her new surroundings for a little while."

Now Henry got down to serious horse training, putting on leather chaps and spurs on his boots. He walked to the horse, let her check him out, slipped on a halter, and began leading her around, mostly letting his body move the horse. He stopped the hose by pressing against her with his front shoulder. Henry gestured to her shoulder point and hip point. He said, "The horse is never wrong; the human is." Henry made the horse put her head down; then he got down on his knees and talked to her.

A horse trainer's proverbs

Henry said horses grow faster than humans and also learn faster. "It's the simple things. Her eyes follow her ears. Watch her eyes. They go soft as the horse learns."

Henry slapped his chaps, and soon the horse didn't mind. He led the horse around in circles, going left, then right, only by changing the rope and with hardly any voice. Soon the horse relaxed. Henry said, "Never let a horse get the upper hand. Fix the little things." Henry made "Shh-shh" sounds. Soon the horse didn't mind.

"Now here's the hard part," Henry said. "This is the most diffi-cult. Train the driver. Don't let the hands do what the mind says. Learn to be gentle; don't use force."

Next, the crew laid a big piece of clear plastic out on the ground. Henry led the horse past it, first six feet away, then closer. Eventu-ally, Henry moved the horse very close to the plastic. The horse was to walk over the plastic. First she jumped over it, then soon she stepped on it, front feet first, then her back feet, and stopped. Henry rubbed the plastic over the horse and finally draped it over her, then slapped her with a whip. The horse didn't mind at all.

Henry said that "horse trainer" is not a good title. "We're not horse trainers. The horse trains us."

Henry made the horse back up by pushing his hands at the horse's eyes. Henry also flexed the horse's neck down. He was very generous with patting and rubbing her neck.

We were at the training on a postcard-picture-perfect, mild spring day. From Jonas Riehl's hilltop farm, one has a panoramic view of eastern Lancaster County. From south to the mine ridge, to the Ephrata Mountain in the north, and then east to the Welsh Mountains, it's a beautiful scene.

About 20 attended this clinic. We were all quite different, except that we were all horse devotees. There were three team Mennonite girls and their brother, several young Amish women, and Jonas Riehl's wife and their daughter with her three small tots, all of us taking in everything we could about horses. Jonas's wife's hands were busy *petzing coppa*, a time-consuming activity necessary to shape our Lancaster Amish women's prayer coverings. But most folks attending were serious about training horses.

Henry brought in his pet horse and demonstrated how a horse responds when Henry shifted his weight in the saddle. He used his legs to press against the horse's sides to make it move sideways. Through all of this, the horse had no bridle on.

These sessions lasted until 11:30 or so, and then it was lunchtime for the people and the animals.

Teaching control

In the afternoon, they put a wild Morgan in a round pen. Two helpers roped the horse around its body in front of its hind legs, and then the show began. The horse ran around the pen for 40 minutes or so until it was out of breath. Even the trainers were sweating.

My horse was next. They carefully placed a blanket and saddle on her. They gave great care to make sure the saddle girths were correctly set. Dave Lee, one of the helpers, prepared to mount her, first pulling her neck around hard. "This locks her transmission," he said. Slowly, Dave stepped into the stirrup on one side, while keeping her head pulled hard to the left. Then he reached over on the other side and flopped the right side stirrup. After 10 minutes or so, Dave finally mounted her completely, still keeping her head turned hard. "Never let a horse start going as you mount," he cautioned. Slowly he released her so she could move.

If she got unruly, he pulled her head around.

Dave spent half an hour making circles, stopping and starting often. Another helper brought out the plastic, and at first the horse spooked. But she soon accepted the plastic being rubbed all over her.

Fear and noise on the road

Then the action changed. Dave walked over to the barn and roared out with a big Case I H tractor, driving it to the large arena so horse and tractor could meet each other. First, the horse was permitted to smell the tractor. Then Dave slowly rode the horse around the machine. The horse relaxed and walked beside the tractor. Next, David started the tractor, roaring it a bit. The horse was quite scared, and when Dave drove it past the machine, it kept its distance. This went on for a half-hour or so. David drove the tractor in circles and reverses. The horse was ridden past the tractor head on, going by slowly. The horse was ridden closer, eventually walking right behind the tractor.

This session lasted over an hour. Dave, every inch a 20-year-old, looked a bit bored. His shirttail hung out, his hair was disheveled, but he was a completely devoted horse trainer, continuing to drive the horse in tight circles. The horse was accepting the tractor better, but its time with the tractor was not over.

Next, my horse was harnessed and hitched to a heavy two-wheeled, rubber-tired training cart with brakes. The horse's bridle had no blinds. Dave Riehl drove the horse into the ring while the tractor was driven past the horse, and then the horse was driven past the tractor. A helper stood in the ring, waving a flag to scare my horse. She got a bit unruly, but soon accepted the tractor, although she never wanted to get close. Soon she was able to ignore the flag.

Dave Lee made big circles forward and backward on the tractor, roaring its motor. Dave Riehl drove my horse past the tractor again and again, each time a bit closer. Soon the horse seemed relaxed, but she still didn't want to get as close to the tractor as David wanted.

Meanwhile, over in the round pen, a big black mule was being brought in. No one dared to go in its stall; even pro horse trainer Jonas stood on the fence to put its halter and rope on. This mule was 1600 pounds of trouble. He had recently knocked his master down, which is why he was hustled off to this clinic. The mule took off running, round and round. Helper Daniel held its rope as the mule kept running in circles, its eyes telling it all. Even Henry Hershberger didn't like the looks of this mule. The helper was working up a sweat. The mule was going to require a very long session.

Finally, Dave Riehl drove my horse out of the ring and came over to me. "We're ready to take your horse out on the road and have the tractor come toward us." Some young girls graciously volunteered to keep my notebook until I got back. I was a little worried about how this would work.

We headed across Route 340 on Weavertown Road, and the tractor came roaring toward us. The horse dashed off the road. Dave showed me how to pull back hard, then release a bit. We turned around and went north this time. The tractor turned around, too, and came toward us again. This time the horse still spooked, but maybe not as much. We repeated this drill about a dozen times. Finally, it was almost 5:00 and time to head back. The horse had a bit better feel for big traffic, but she wasn't as comfortable with the tractor as I hoped.

When we got back to Jonas Riehl's, the mule-training was still going on. There was more of an audience now; the young girls were taking in every one of the trainer's moves.

As I hitched up my horse and drove home, I reflected on the day. The fee to bring a horse for training was $165.00. For that money, my horse was given over six hours of training of many different kinds. She and I gained a lot of helpful hints about how to cope with traffic stress.

Have a problem horse? Contact Jonas Riehl or Henry Hershberger!

CHAPTER TWENTY-THREE

Hosting Church

Who decides the schedule for hosting church, and what happens when it's your turn?

The standard procedure is that after the benediction at our Sunday morning worship service, the deacon announces, *"In twe Vocha iss dee fasumling un's Sam Stoltzfus'sa."* (In two weeks we will gather at Sam Stoltzfuses.) It is religiously significant and a blessing to host the worship service on your property.

Services can be held on the main floor of the house or in the basement or shop. And so for the next two weeks, the whole family is geared to getting ready for church. A visit from the U.S. President or the Queen of England wouldn't stir as much excitement as getting ready for the worship service at your home.

Cleaning and cleaning

We Old Order Amish can tend to be a bit envious of the horse-and-buggy Mennonites who hold their services in their large meetinghouses without the stress of getting ready for church. But for us, the barn gets a complete cleaning, cobwebs are knocked down, box-stall manure is hauled out, and windows are washed. If necessary, the white-washer comes to coat the horse and cow stable. (This is also a board of health requirement if the farmer is shipping Class 1 milk.)

In the house, Mam and the daughters, and maybe a hired girl, are busy cleaning the whole place, washing windows inside and out, and maybe giving a quick coat of paint to a room or two. If it's a young couple who's hosting, without older children to help, the neighbors will pitch in to help with the cleaning.

At times when there's been a death in the family of the hosting household, and they have to be with the mourners, the whole neighborhood kicks into a Class 1 alert and helps get the place ready for church. It takes a little planning, but usually several close neighbor women make the pies. A half-dozen women or teen-age girls clean the room where the services will be held. Several close neighborhood men set up the benches and chairs on Saturday afternoon. Come Sunday morning, the place is church-ready. Often there are tears of thankfulness and appreciation when the resident family comes back and sees what has taken place.

The bench wagon

After the previous worship service concludes, the next host inquires about the bench wagon schedule. Will the wagon be available when it is needed in two weeks at the next place of worship? The family in any district who will host church the next time has first rights to the district's bench wagon. If all is routine, the family who just hosted the services will take the wagon in the next several days to where the next scheduled worship service will be held. However, Murphy's Law can apply here. If a funeral or wedding or benefit auction or youth group gathering is planned in the next two weeks, the bench wagon may be needed there, and so may not show up until the day before the Sunday services. Sometimes the wagon may be so far away that it's easier to borrow a neighboring district's wagon so the benches can be set up on a more relaxed schedule.

After the Sunday service, those women who are close neighbors to the woman who will host the next service often offer to bring the homemade whole wheat bread or the cup cheese or pretzels for the fellowship meal. If the hostess is a mother with a small baby, more women will volunteer to help get ready.

Food prep

As the final countdown looms near, the hostess and several neighbors get together and make some 50 snitz pies, usually on the Friday or Saturday morning before the services. They store the pies in a special pie chest that travels with the bench wagon.

Snitz pies are a Lancaster County church staple and a must for the fellowship meal. Some innovative women will add pumpkin pies or Christmas cookies during the Christmas season. This is not a meal for calorie watchers, but eating a piece or two of snitz pie once every two weeks won't add much to one's waistline.

Snitz Pie recipe for 20 pies

2 teaspoons ground cinnamon

1 teaspoon ground nutmeg

¼ cup minute tapioca

½ teaspoon ground cloves

2 teaspoons salt

5 cups sugar

2 gallons applesauce

5 cups apple butter

Lemon extract or juice, to taste

20 unbaked pie crusts, plus top crusts

1. Mix the seasonings and tapioca with the sugar.
2. Stir in the applesauce and apple butter (a timesaver instead of using dried apple slices).
3. Add lemon extract or juice to taste.
4. Divide the filling mixture among the 20 pie crusts. Cover each filled crust with a top crust.
5. Bake at 425° for 15 minutes; then at 350° for 30 minutes.

If the hostess is busy with farming, or in the middle of summer gardening, she can go to the local bakery and order the snitz pies for a modest outlay of $3.00 to $5.00 per pie.

Every host family knows they need to have at least several pounds of coffee on hand. Some hostesses also serve hot chocolate and tea. During the meal, three women go around, each with a coffee pot in hand to serve their guests.

On Saturday afternoon, the yard and flowerbeds get a final going over, and the driveway is swept. If it's winter and there's snow, the driveway will be plowed. Finally, by bedtime all is ready, and the whole family is glad for rest.

On Sunday morning, everyone in the family gets up early, does their chores quickly, eats breakfast in a hurry, and dresses in their Sunday best. If all goes as planned, everything is ready by 7:00 a.m. But sick children, frozen pipes, or a water pump failure can play havoc with carefully made plans. Soon after 7:00, the district's families start to arrive.

Who might come?

Something we enjoy in our districts of 20 to 30 families each is that there are always visitors at our Sunday morning services. Ministers, family members, and visitors from other districts—from a 20-mile radius and other states—come to worship with us. We always look forward to seeing who the visitors will be. Hopefully a visiting minister will come and preach; it's always interesting to hear the gospel from a different voice, a kind of first-class, plain-folk revival meeting. The younger children watch for some of their faraway cousins among the visitors. By 7:45, most of the teams have arrived; the horses are unhitched and stabled. Soon after 8:00, all the congregation is seated, and the worship service starts with the announcement of the first hymn. There may be some latecomers; they will sit wherever there is room.

First is a short opening sermon, then a prayer, followed by the main sermon and a long prayer.

After the benediction and the announcement about the location of the next service, the congregation sings a final hymn, and worship is over. The single boys and girls file out, and then there is such a flurry of activity, that it's a bit hard to follow. Even the best planned political caucus would seem slow by comparison.

Efficiency...

Several older men collect the *Ausbund* hymn books and put them in the book boxes. The host gives the young men orders about which length benches to set up for the tables. Trestles which were leaning along the walls are placed, the benches are set in them, and presto, the tables are set up. A woman rolls out a long, white, paper tablecloth and snips it off at the end. At Christmas-time, a colored tablecloth may be used. The young girls move so efficiently to set the tables that Marriott waiters would be put to shame. The pie chest is rolled in, pies and bread, cheese and peanut butter are set out, along with pickles, red beets, and pretzels. The fellowship meal is ready.

The men and women are seated at the tables in the same order they came into the service that morning. The resident bishop or head minister leads a silent blessing. Immediately, several women and girls go around to the tables and ask each person if they want tea or coffee. After all are finished eating, another silent grace is given at the end of the meal.

If there's not enough room for everyone to sit down to eat at the first sitting, the women and girls hustle to set up a dishwashing station, washing dishes much faster than any electric dishwasher ever did. When everyone has eaten, the tables are cleared and the remaining dishes are washed. The worship service is not considered complete until the fellowship meal is over.

... and relaxed visiting

Then the men and women sit around and visit, the men discussing the latest political maneuvers and the price of mules or horses or farms. The women talk about cooking, gardens, concerns about their babies, or who is ill and needs help in the next weeks. Then most of the congregation heads home. Close neighbors and relatives stay for supper. The hostess, with several helpers, sets the tables and puts out a spread to equal the finest banquets.

If there are *Rumspringa* in the family, the youth may gather for the supper, too, followed by a hymn sing in the evening. This means that about 60 to 80 youth and some of their parents will come, starting in the early afternoon. This coincides well with hosting church since the place is all cleaned up, the house has been prepared for the church service, and the barn is cleared for the horses. If the weather is right, there will be several volleyball games, or corner-ball games in the barn if it's rainy. The benches and tables can be re-set for supper, and the benches for the hymn sing. The book box containing the *Unpartheyisches Gesangbuchs* needed for the youth singing is on the bench wagon.

The hymn sing starts at 7:00 and is over by 9:00. Then a snack is served, and by 10:00, everyone has left.

It makes a long day, but there is a blessing in having the worship service and providing a gathering place for youth activities in your home.

CHAPTER TWENTY-FOUR

All Aboard for a Buggy Ride to Church

I'd like to invite you to travel with us by horse and buggy on a 20-mile drive to an Amish worship service. It's a Sunday morning in early spring. Our buggy is a standard Lancaster County Amish carriage, 39 inches wide and 72 inches long, with hydraulic brakes, 12-volt lights and turning signals, and windows for cold-weather riding. It's not the roomiest, but it's a fun way to see the country. There's time to smell the roses as you go.

A journey like this takes a bit of preparation the day before. On Saturday, we thoroughly washed the carriage. We gave the blankets a good shaking and aired them out on the washline. We also checked the battery and brake fluid and used some cleaner to make the windows sparkle. Next, we curried our horse, George W. Bush, cleaned his feet, and oiled his hooves so they were nice and soft. I checked the harness, and we were set.

At 4:00 a.m. Sunday, I fed George and ran the curry comb over his coat once more. "Easy, George," I said as I threw the harness on his back.

Sunday best

After a quick breakfast, we put on our traditional Sunday best—a white shirt, black suit, hat, and overcoat for me, and a dress, black bonnet, and shawl for my wife. I bridled George, hitched him to the carriage, and ran the reins through the window holes. With a mug of coffee on the dash, we were off at 5:10. We stopped to pick up my parents. They're in their 80s, have vision loss, and don't drive anymore. I let George walk out of their lane and held him back a bit as we started down the road. Best to start slow.

"It's a nice Sunday morning," I commented in German. The temperature was about 30 degrees with a mild breeze out of the west. George soon warmed up and trotted along at a steady 10 miles an hour. *Dat* and I talked up front, while *Mam* and Katie chatted in the back.

On a long trip like this, you don't select the shortest route. Rather, you pick the roads with the fewest hills. After a while, I let George rest a bit. We still had six miles to go. Clip-clopping a little further up the road, we entered Mennonite country. Their black carriages with wide doors differ from our gray Amish carriages. Again, I let George catch his breath as we stopped to visit with a Mennonite man walking to a meetinghouse for services.

We continued north on Reading Road, and by then we could see many other Amish carriages with horses trotting along, their breaths forming gray clouds in the morning sun.

Worship service

We were heading for the home of my sister and her husband, the Melvin Kings, where our worship service would be held in their wood shop. It was 7:30 when we got there, and I let George walk up the lane to the horse barn. After the 20-mile, two-hour trip, he wasn't even breathing hard. Melvin's daughters rushed out to greet their grandparents, while Melvin put George away. "Don't give him too much water, please," I cautioned.

Church started at 8:00 and adjourned at 11:00. We enjoyed a traditional fellowship meal afterwards, of snitz pies, red beets, pickles, bread, and coffee. I checked on George at noon to make sure he'd been fed and watered, and then went back to more visiting. At 2:30, we hitched up the carriage and headed home on a different route, stopping at some friends' home for supper. That gave George an hour to rest.

It was sundown when we got home. Now George could really rest a spell.

CHAPTER TWENTY-FIVE

Some Thoughts about Choosing a Cemetery Plot

They say there are three things in life everyone should have: a will, a family doctor, and a cemetery plot. You will need all of them, but for many of us, they aren't on the front burner till later in life. But that's not the wisest. As soon as you're responsible for yourself, you should have a doctor who will care for you and keep your records on file. And as soon as you have personal property or real estate, you should have a will.

But even for us traditional Amish who bury in cemeteries, when to choose your cemetery plot can be a matter of choice. Yet life is full of surprises. Sometimes a young couple suddenly loses a child, or a relatively young adult dies, and then a cemetery plot must be chosen quickly.

First, let me say that I am thankful that our Amish churches conduct our funerals and burials as our parents did for many generations. I give thanks to the good Lord and our government for this privilege and hope it will continue for our descendants.

I have been a cemetery caretaker for our Gordonville Amish cemetery for over 30 years, and I have a few pointers about cemetery regulations, should you ever need such a service. If I give useful advice, thank the Lord, not me. If I give incorrect advice, I ask to be forgiven.

Have you thought about how most cemeteries are laid out and managed? Here in the Gordonville graveyard, a three-man board assists in locating graves, plans the summertime mowing schedule, and sees that necessary repairs are made. This cemetery was started by the Jacob Weaver family in late 1700. The first burials were in the 1720s. In 1812, 16 Amish families purchased the first section.

Thinking like a cemetery caretaker

The standard cemetery lot is 102″ wide and 210″ long. This is for five 42″ wide graves. The reason for creating lots of five graves is that in the old days, many families lost one or two small children, or at times the husband or wife passed away, and there would be a second marriage. Thus another grave could be needed. In such circumstances, three graves could be quickly filled, and two would remain for the parent couple or unmarried children.

I'm often asked, "What are proper cemetery manners?" In my more than 20 years of assisting folks to pick out a gravesite for a family member, I've found there is no set procedure about how to make a decision, but some approaches are more satisfactory than others. I've seen so many different ways that families decide on a gravesite.

For the first death in a family, it's always best, and easiest for the cemetery caretaker, if one of the parents comes along to the cemetery. If it's an older parent that is to be buried, it's good if several children come to help decide on the spot for the grave. This is very important in the case of an accidental, sudden death because often folks need guidance at such a sorrowful time. I recall one incident when a 12-year-old son died in a fire, and the whole family of parents and nine children came. I've seen several cases of infant deaths where both sets of grandparents came with the parents of the deceased and provided support. This makes the cemetery man's task so much easier.

As a rule, folks will contact the cemetery man and ask him to meet the family, as well as the gravediggers, at an appointed time. This is especially helpful in cold or stormy weather. So folks, please keep in mind that cemetery caretakers are usually busy people with work to do, and they appreciate if cemetery appointments are kept in a timely way.

Now, just for the record, there can be some trying situations in cemetery duties. Some years ago, a family suffered the death of an infant child. Apparently their schedule was limited, and their parents may not have been available. So they sent two men from their church to me with these instructions: "Tell Sam to pick out a lot and a gravesite."

"Well," I said, "will my choice be correct and proper for them?"

All that the men could say was that they had been so instructed. So we went out to the cemetery and made a choice.

The complications of choosing a plot

One of the more complicated times in my experience was when a young mother died, and the gravediggers came to me with these instructions: "Tell Sam to pick out a lot for the young wife and also for the grandparents."

I knew the family fairly well and knew that the deceased had an older single brother who would someday need grave space. The family would take five or six grave sites if a second wife eventually needed to be buried in the plot. So I told the gravediggers I needed to talk with the grandparents before I made a choice.

While the gravediggers waited, I went to a nearby phone, contacted the family, and pointed out the need for six graves. The grandparents had earlier planned to be buried in their own family plot, but they agreed to my suggestion. After an hour's delay, the gravediggers could make the grave. Here again, if one of the family members had been present at the cemetery, a choice could have been made in a more timely manner.

I understand that these trying situations often happen because folks in sorrow can't always make the best decisions. And yet some folks still insist on old customs. Let me illustrate with a case from some years ago. Two men came quite late on a Saturday evening with the request for a gravesite for a small child who had just died. Since it was still daylight, and there would have been time, I suggested they dig the grave right away. "No," they said, "the family plans to do it tomorrow," which was Sunday. Oh! I asked when the funeral would be. "Also tomorrow, and plans are to make the grave when the family gets to the cemetery."

Since it always takes time to select a new lot, I did it that Saturday evening just as the sun set, since the next day was our church Sunday.

This is what happened next. When the family and the ministers came to the cemetery for the burial, the gravediggers made the grave. It took a bit longer than usual because the weather had been dry and the digging was slow. The whole group waited until the grave was made, and then the burial was completed. Delaying the digging of the grave until the time of the burial also made our local undertaker frown a bit. I don't recommend making a grave at the time of burial.

It's a bit hard to know what to say when a family comes to find a gravesite, especially if they are some of my old friends. In one case, I received a phone call to select a grave site for a year-old child. The parents were quite young. They wanted it near the grandparents' plot. So I went quite early and laid out the gravesite which I thought would fit well. However, the young parents wished to have a site near a shade tree. I could understand that this would offer some comfort, so I found another plot near the shade tree the parents desired. There wasn't much extra time involved, but

I had to make sure a five-grave lot was available there.

Sensitive situations

Another thing to keep in mind—are any of the deceased's family no longer Amish? If a space is to be available to bury a family member who has drifted away from the faith, this must be discussed ahead of time and agreed to by the family. Several persons who didn't lead Amish lives and died in their later years are buried here in the Gordonville cemetery.

Another situation needs to be addressed in any graveyard, including here in Gordonville. Several families buried family members here by opening a five-grave lot. Then they moved to another county or state. What is to be done with the remaining spaces? It would be courteous if such families planned ahead and communicated with the cemetery caretaker about what is to be done with the remaining spaces.

Uncertainty happens in a cemetery as in any part of life. Some years ago a husband died and was buried here at Gordonville. Later the wife left the Amish faith. When she passed away, she was buried in her current church's cemetery. Should the husband, who had been buried some 10 years earlier, be exhumed and placed beside his wife in her churchyard cemetery?

Just recently a husband and his second wife were both killed when a car hit their carriage. Only the husband's children came to me to see about burying their parents. So we planned to place the father beside his first wife. The next grave over was filled with a small child the couple had buried years before. So the second wife was buried two spaces away from her husband. The family all seemed agreed.

About two weeks after the burial, the wife's family decided it would be more proper to bury their mother beside her first husband in their local cemetery 15 miles away. So a day was chosen and the gravediggers made a new grave. Then the family came to Gordonville, opened the grave, exhumed their mother, and buried her beside her first husband. At the time of such a sudden death, families can be in a state of shock and may make decisions that they later question.

Keeping good records

I have more stories, but my intention here is to encourage good communication, to treat everyone involved respectfully, and to keep proper records. Each caretaker should have a record book, and they should all be kept up-to-date.

When new cemeteries are planned, it is important to make a layout plan and have each space numbered. And to all folks, please bear with the cemetery caretakers. They are only human and can make mistakes. Burials can be done in the wrong place, and it is sometimes hard to make corrections. It's happened to me. On at least one occasion, we had no choice but to bury a person in another place because their designated space was filled.

Once at Ronks cemetery, a boy was buried in the wrong space. When the family discovered this, the deceased was moved the next day.

Cemetery care can be rewarding, especially if all the families work together. One of our Gordonville cemetery caretakers, Levi Fisher, used to be very appreciative of all who helped with mowing and repairs and would say thank you over and over again.

So we should do today. We must appreciate all those who help with the cemetery work.

All Amish social events, including weddings and funerals, happen in members' homes and farm buildings. The school is the only other building where Amish life occurs.

The Amish do not fly, so that they remain close to their families, church, and local community. But they are permitted to travel by ship, train, and bus.

The Amish trace their start to the Protestant Reformation in Europe in the 1520s, specifically the groups known as Anabaptists. The Amish began in 1693, the date when they broke with the Mennonites around concerns about faithfulness.

CHAPTER TWENTY-SIX

Living in the *Doddyhaus*; Our Semi-Retired Years

We all know how it works, yet it still feels mysterious when you join the grandparents group. I've tried to do it carefully. Officially, we became grandparents when our oldest son and his wife had their first child in 1992. By then our second son was married, and he wanted to take over the farming. So that winter we made plans to make a *Doddyhaus*. I drew a blueprint and took it to the township leaders to get a permit. We began building—it took most of the winter—and by early spring, our second son and his wife moved in. Since we still had six children at home, we stayed in the farm house; our son and daughter-in-law occupied the *Doddyhaus*. It was quite a change not to do the milking and morning and evening chores, but now I could pursue my woodworking business and also make horseradish. And I often helped our son with the farming.

Preparing to host a wedding

That same fall, our oldest daughter was planning to get married, so we found ourselves in the whirlwind of preparing to host our first wedding. We had started getting ready in the early spring, and we didn't have to give any orders twice! The work went like magic. We fixed those things that were necessary, and even some that seemed a bit extravagant. Our daughter went around painting the house windows. The shop roof was painted. Fences were painted. And we hired a painter to paint the barn. Our oldest son and wife came home and helped.

Our basement had never been finished, so now we put in a ceiling and painted every surface in the basement. It felt good to see the place all spruced up. We extended the garden so we could plant more potatoes, peas, carrots, and celery. We arranged with a local chicken farmer to supply the fat chickens for the wedding roasts. My wife's sisters came one day to butcher the chickens and store them in the freezer.

The colors of the wedding dresses were chosen and made; the *navasizzers* (best boy and girl) were selected. Things went well, including the wedding day weather. Our daughter had been a school teacher for three years, so it was a big wedding with lots of school parents invited. And now we had a son-in-law.

One joy of having married children was going along with them when they went visiting on weekends, soon after their weddings. They were given lots of wedding presents, and a part of our basement was set up with tables to display the gifts. Just before their moving day, they carefully packed the gifts and took them along to their new home. It's all a part of the process of having married children.

Of course, before the moving day, there was a flurry of furniture-making and gathering of a full line of kitchen gear, including a stove and fridge.

In 1994, our second daughter married, and we repeated the activities—sprucing up the place, fixing, painting, making furniture, and getting them moved into their own home. Things went faster this time because our married children came to help both with the planning and the preparation.

Two years later our third daughter planned to marry, so we did a complete re-run. By now our whole family had a system, and things went quite well. But this wedding was in December on a rainy day. So the house was very crowded since most folks wanted to be inside. Now we had five married children and lots of grandchildren.

Christmas-time has become so special when we have our family for Christmas dinner and give them all gifts. One of the families gave us a special wall hanging—a painted birthday record of the grandchildren's birthdays, with room to add more as they are born, so we can keep track of the birthdays and send each a greeting. It's a good system, but we don't always get the greetings sent on the date we should. No wonder since by now we have *many* grandchildren!

In 2017, our third daughter gave birth to a stillborn child, so there was a funeral, and we laid our 50th grandchild in the grave. It was a very touching ceremony, especially so that now part of our family is in the Lord's hands.

Another family tradition we practice is that on each grandchild's birthday, we stick the required number of candles in a box of ice cream, light the candles, give it to the grandchild and their family, and sing "Happy Birthday." Then the whole family can enjoy the ice cream.

Now's the time

Soon after our third daughter's wedding, we decided to move over to the *Doddyhaus*. Our second son and his family moved into the farm house part since they had two children. Also, they were closer to the barn at that end of the house. Now we were officially retired. We tried to think and behave like proper *doddys* should.

Lots of benefits…

It is nice to be able to take extended weekends and go to our married children overnight. By now our two youngest boys were eight and 10, and they were glad to go along and play with their nieces and nephews. When our oldest daughter and family moved to Wisconsin in 1999, we took family trips to help with their work. In 2004, they moved to Kentucky, so we've made many trips to the Bluegrass state, again to help with their work. In 2015 and in 2017, their oldest sons married. Both times, we hired a charter bus, and many family and friends made the 700-mile trip with us. We stayed overnight, took in the wedding, and came home the next day. It's a great blessing to see one's grandchildren marry in the faith and start their own homes.

…and responsibilities

We try, too, to be proper grandparents in our district by visiting the elderly. I'm among the five oldest men in the district, and sometimes when the ministers face a complex church situation, we're asked for advice. When there are neighborhood disasters or funerals, Katie and I go to offer assistance and condolences. As grandparents, there are times we can offer financial aid to those in need. And if a family has large medical expenses, we help to plan a benefit auction and help at the auction itself.

We are next-door neighbors to our Amish Library, so I spend

many Saturdays there as Librarian and also assisting in planning tours. I give a lot of hours, too, helping at the Lancaster Mennonite Historical Society. It feels good to have the time, resources, and health to pursue such activities.

I took another journey not many Amish grandparents get to take in July of 2016, through the urging of a long-time friend, Mennonite historian John Ruth. I, along with 18 other Amish, made a five-week trip to places connected with Anabaptist history in Belgium, France, Holland, Germany, Switzerland, Austria, and England. We crossed the Atlantic on the Queen Mary 2, toured Europe for three weeks and London for a day, and then returned home on the QM2. I do not think of it as a pleasure trip, since we visited many places where our Anabaptist forebears suffered terrible persecution. We visited some 30 places mentioned in our 400-year-old *Ausbund* church hymnal.

Another grandfather adventure which I do that is a bit unusual is publish several books. So as you see, Amish grandfathers don't just sit around. They stay busy and help others. Grandparent life is, in many ways, what one makes of it—full of joys and surprises, and at times sorrows.

In 2016, our oldest married grandson and his wife had a baby daughter. So at ages 74 and 70, Katie and I have stepped into a new group—great-grandparents!

CHAPTER TWENTY-SEVEN

A History of the Gordonville Fire Company Sale, aka a Mud Sale

Early in the spring of 1969, Gordonville Fire Chief Jake Herr made an unusual proposal. "Let's have a consignment sale to raise funds for the fire company." He dubbed it a white elephant sale. So began a tradition that endures to this day. Ed Klimuska, a Lancaster Newspaper reporter, gave this spring-time sale, and other neighboring ones, the title, "Mud Sale," which they have often turned out to be.

In the first years of the sale, proceeds were not spectacular and involved relatively little labor. The sale began on the fire hall property along Vigilant St., but by the late '70s, it had spread over to Ted Cardwell's fields at 191 Maple St. and Jake Fisher's

Pequea Machine Yards. As the sale expanded and more goods were sold, more parking spaces were needed. The sale by then covered much of East Gordonville and parking was in the fields.

By the mid-80s, Jake Fisher, weary of all the wear and tear on his property, requested that the sale be held in the fire hall area and the field west of Leacock Road. (Jake had purchased part of that property from Walter Kellemberger.) That continues to be its location today. Around 1996, shuttle busses were hired to drive around to local parking lots to pick up sale-goers and transport them to the sale.

In 1992, the practice began to close Leacock Road on sale day. Each year the sale continued to be larger and management got better. By 2005, sales topped the million dollar mark.

Along the way, a serious problem developed with the corner ball game that took place alongside the sale. A fence got damaged. Then a kindhearted farmer in Soudersburg offered the use of his barn for the corner ball games. Folks could ride the sale shuttle buses to get there.

Successful community project

Today the sale committee consists of some 16 persons. Over 250 volunteers help to unload, sell, and load the consignments. During sale days, over 15 auctioneers are selling at any time. Thanks to Jake Herr's idea, this sale generates funds to keep the local fire and ambulance equipment updated. This yearly event, along with the fall lumber and buggy sale, tie the community together like a modern-day miracle. It will soon be in its 50th year.

Through the years, sale days have been fairly routine—some were rainy or snowy, and many were beautifully sunny. But no one was prepared for what the March 13, 1993 sale day would bring. It had been a mild late winter, the farmers were plowing, and the weather was spring-like as we got ready for the sale. The day before the sale, a big snowstorm was forecast. Well, storms had been predicted before that hadn't happened, so just maybe the weatherman would be wrong again. Friday evening, calls began rolling in. "Are you gonna have the sale?" My dad Gideon was manning the phones. "Yes, we plan to have the sale." Several busloads of out-of-state quilt buyers stopped in to inspect the quilts. They were planning to stay overnight at nearby motels. However, they never left the motel the next day, and some were stranded until March 16th.

Uh-oh

The snow came very softly Saturday morning, like a cat tip-toeing in the garden. First, there were little flakes. At 8:00, it began to snow for real. The sale started as usual, and in the tents, business was normal. But outside, things were fast becoming a nightmare. Consignment sheets were suddenly snow-covered, the wind was picking up, tickets were blowing away. Even with an umbrella holder for each clerk, it was fast becoming impossible to write because fingers were freezing. Then the Leacock Township snowplow crew stopped in and recommended halting the sale because it was quickly becoming impossible to keep the roads open.

The sales committee held an emergency meeting and soon made an announcement over the loudspeakers: "The sale is cancelled. Anyone who is able, please help take down the tents." The 40 mile-an-hour winds were ripping them up. For the rest of the morning, dozens of men loaded up the sale goods from under the tents onto Hoober Feed trucks, which hauled everything over to Hoober Feeds' truck garage. All the tents were eventually laid down.

Many people struggled through the snow to get home. Several locals with snowmobiles and four-wheel-drive vehicles ferried many folks home. By early evening, the snow turned to freezing rain, and the wind picked up to 60 miles an hour. By then, travel was next to impossible. A pettibone was used to take sale helpers home who lived more than two miles away.

The sale was rescheduled for the next Friday, March 19. The tents went back up, and the goods were finally sold. But the bookwork was a nightmare, with all the missing tickets, unreadable consignment sheets, and lost buyers' numbers. However, as always before, the Gordonville volunteer spirit was as dependable as ever, and hundreds of hours were donated until the office work was done.

The Amish—men and women alike—actively support relief and disaster efforts sponsored by Mennonite charities with their time, carpentry, quilting, and sewing skills, and their money. They have done this for many, many years.

CHAPTER TWENTY-EIGHT

Canning Turkey Meat in the Lower Pequea

The lights go on early during canning week at the John Freemen Stoltzfus farm near Narvon, some two miles east of the village of White Horse. At 3:00 in the morning, the first shift arrives, usually four 14-passenger van loads, bringing some 50 men and boys.

The meat is brought out in tubs and emptied onto long tables. Sleepy-eyed men line up at the tables and start cutting the three- to five-pound turkey meat chunks into bite-size pieces. A long shelf above each table holds whetstones for sharpening the knives as they get dull. Each married man has a beard, so each one is given a white beard cover to wear. And everyone must wear a white butcher's apron.

As the cutting begins, so does the conversation. What do four van loads of Amish men from different church districts—who don't see each other often or maybe don't know each other—talk about?! Lots of stories, maybe some gossip, certainly lots of interesting discourses.

An assembly line for good

This meat canning operation is overseen by the Mennonite Central Committee (MCC). It began after World War II. The first canner was made in Hesston, Kansas. At first the meat was canned in glass containers, but there was too much breakage. Metal containers were found to be more durable. The government scoffed at the idea of operating a mobile canner, so the Mennonite churches took hold and started the project. The original canner has been replaced several times; the current one was built in 1993.

The mobile canner is mounted on a semi-trailer with fold-out sides. A crew of six to 10 men work in the trailer. The cut up meat is carried out to the canner, heated to the proper temperature, put into cans, sealed, and then loaded into a Retort, which is a large pressure cooker. There the meat is pressure-cooked for 135 minutes. Then the cans are cooled in flowing cold water until they're safe to handle. Next, a different crew hand-washes, dries, inspects, labels, and puts the cans in boxes. The filled boxes are stacked on pallets and incubated in a warehouse to make sure they're safe before distributing them around the world to those in need.

Around 5:30, word comes that it's breakfast-time. About half the workers go downstairs to eat. The cutting goes on; when the first group returns, the rest go for breakfast. It is a busy scene: three tables of cutters, another group washing cans, several pappies back in the corner sticking labels onto cans, with the ingredients and production and expiration dates clearly visible.

Three shifts each day

At 8:30 we get orders to clean up. We scrape and wash all the cutting tables with steaming hot water. Then beard covers and aprons go off, and the first shift files downstairs. At nine o'clock, the second shift starts. They'll work until three o'clock. Downstairs, a full staff of younger girls and women operate a lunch stand. All morning long, part of this crew packs school lunches to be delivered to local Amish schools. During this week, over 1200 school lunches will be prepared as a fundraiser to finance the canner's operations. Approximately 120 beef cattle, costing some $15,000.00, are prepared in the canner each day. Since beef is so high-priced, turkey is more often chosen. Freewill donations are also collected in all the Lancaster County Amish church districts to help pay for the meat and for the canner upkeep.

At 2:45, the second shift of workers begins cleanup. And at 2:45 in the afternoon, vans start rolling in King Road, bringing the third shift. Empty vans also pull in to take the second shift home. The evening shift works until 8:30, when the cleanup gang arrives. They will dismiss at nine p.m.

Great care is continually given to meet all the cleanliness and cooking temperature codes. Mid-morning, inspectors dressed in butcher whites and wearing white hard hats make a thorough check of all quarters. Brownie Dave and his boys also make sure the rules are kept, insisting that everyone is wearing butcher aprons and that all beard covers are on. I made a serious misdemeanor, one that is contrary to the canner's rules. I left my butcher apron on when I went to the bathroom, which didn't miss Brownie Dave's sharp eyes. "Hey, chuck that apron and get a new one!" I was embarrassed and sorry.

Thanks to the Loren and Wanda Yoder family of Belleville, Pennsylvania, who traveled with the canner for one year and wrote an informative, 110-page book (*Together We Can*), describing the canner's travels in the 2008-2009 season. Every year, a different family travels in a camper with the canner as it goes its many miles.

This MCC canner operation is serious business and is not run as a hobby. In the 2008-2009 season, between October and April, the canner made 38 set-ups in 12 states and two stops in Canada, processing 956,787 cans of meat. That provided over 13 million meals for families with low incomes or maybe no income. At Narvon, about 180 men helped each day, for a total of over 900 men and boys donating their time to help.

In the New Testament book of Matthew, chapter 25, Jesus said, "I was hungry and you gave me meat." Thanks to the Christian teaching in our plain churches, some of the hungry are being fed. And when we do it "for the least of these," the Bible reminds us that we are doing it for Jesus. This wording is on each can of meat processed by those who work with the MCC canner: "In the name of Christ." Let's pray that this canning operation continues for many generations.

The tragedy at the Amish school in Nickel Mines, Pennsylvania, drew the attention of the world because of its horror, but perhaps primarily because of the way the Amish responded—in an attitude of forgiveness.

CHAPTER TWENTY-NINE

The Nickel Mines Tragedy Some Years Later

Down in Bart Township along White Oak Road, about 600 feet west of the Mine Road intersection, is a strip of asphalt on the north side of the road, evidence that a driveway entrance was once there. It was where the lane to West Nickel Mines School began. Nearby in the meadow stands a single maple tree. It stood on the west side of the one-room Amish school. These are the only tangible reminders of the schoolhouse at that location.

The school day started that fateful Monday morning, October 2, 2006, as any Amish school day would. Teacher Emma Zook, 22 years old, probably arrived about 7:00 a.m. She unlocked the door, opened the windows, and spent some 30 minutes doing final planning for the school day. It was a warm autumn day; the sunrise foretold a sunny day to come. The school followed the Pennsylvania school code, which stipulates 180 school days per year, with six hours each day.

In a one-mile radius around the school, mothers packed lunches and saw their children off with hearty good-byes. The Sunday before had been the Fall Council Meeting worship services, which is for members only, so many of the children hadn't seen their schoolmates the day before in church.

About 7:30 the school children started arriving at the West Nickel Mines School. "Good morning, Teacher," the pupils greeted their teacher, who replied to each pupil by name and with a hearty "Good morning." Four women from the teacher's family arrived to visit the school.

At 8:00 the teacher rang the bell, and the children dashed to take their seats. Teacher Emma started the school day by reading Acts 4 from the Bible. Then all the pupils rose and said the Lord's Prayer in German. The students moved to the space in front of the blackboard, stood in rows, and sang four or five songs. This was more music than usual because they had guests.

The morning went by quickly. The visitors looked at the school diary and art work, signed the school's guest book, and watched the teacher conduct classes. Then it was time for the 15-minute morning recess. The pupils ran out to play—baseball for the upper grades, and hopscotch, tag, and jump rope for the little ones. Often Teacher Emma helped to play baseball.

But at 10:15, a pickup truck backed up to the schoolhouse door and a horrible event began. What made Mr. Roberts pick the West Nickel Mines School to perform this terrible act? There were four Amish schoolhouses within a one-mile radius. (One blessing would soon emerge—four Amish church districts come together at the Mine Road and White Oak crossroads. That means four sets of ministers were able to care for their charges during the four funerals. And four sets of benches were available to use for the funerals.)

According to Mr. Roberts' list, he had organized all of his plans beforehand. But as he announced his plans to the pupils and visitors, he allowed the visitors and boys to leave. Somehow, the teacher also slipped out, ran one-half mile to the Levi King farm, and phoned for help. Meanwhile, the boys were behind the boys' toilet praying.

Mr. Roberts wanted the blinds drawn, so he went around pulling the roller shades down. One would just snap up again, and Roberts spent considerable time pulling it down. This caused a delay. By the time four state troopers arrived at the school eight or nine minutes later, through lots of traffic and back roads, Roberts had proceeded with his deeds. He had tied up 10 girls with bungee cords and had barricaded all the doors of the school with lumber he brought along.

After Roberts had tied up the girls, there was some touching conversation between them. "Will you pray for me?" he asked.

One of the girls said, "Why don't you pray for us?" Roberts replied, "I don't believe in prayer."

It appeared that Roberts planned to molest one of the younger girls. The older girls said, *"Du net."* (Don't do it.) Roberts told the girls, "I'm sorry I have to do this, but I'm angry with God because of the death of my firstborn daughter, Elsie." In a suicide note he wrote, "I'm filled with so much hate toward me and God." By then the police had come, and they began talking to Roberts with a bullhorn. There was also a conversation between Roberts and the police via cell phone.

When the girls realized Roberts was going to shoot them, 13-year-old Marian Fisher said, "Shoot me first." At 11:15, Roberts carried out his horrible plans and shot the 10 girls. Five died; five survived. Those who died were Marian; 12-year-old Anna Mae; two sisters: eight-year-old Mary Liz and seven-year-old Lena; seven-year-old Naomi Rose; and Mr. Roberts, who shot himself.

Suddenly the scene along the quiet country road was filled with police cars and ambulances. Helicopters came whirling down, and right on their heels, the media. The first responders performed heroic deeds that day, getting the five survivors into ambulances and helicopters and off to hospitals that could handle multiple gunshot wounds. It seemed unreal. Big-city crime had come to our Amish world. There were many tears. Many ambulance personnel had to brace themselves to stay strong.

The community rises

As soon as the Amish neighborhood within a three- to four-mile radius realized there were four funerals to plan, a multitude of folks came to provide help and support. The funerals were arranged so that the families and school parents involved could attend each one. Men had to be appointed to dig graves, deliver funeral invitations, and decide who was to preach. Barns needed to be cleaned out to accommodate the horses. Undertakers had to plan their schedules so they could handle four Amish funerals. Houses, or barns if the houses weren't large enough, had to be emptied and benches set.

During each of the viewings, meals were brought in for the immediate family. Usher teams often worked from early morning until nine or 10 o'clock in the evening. The cemetery caretaker was busy for four straight days. But God's grace and love were very evident many times. Total strangers and outsiders offered their help as the grieving families and stunned community tried to comprehend what had happened.

On October 9, one week after the shooting, the parents and schoolboys entered the school to get schoolbooks and such. Then the blackboards were torn out to preserve the old slate since it's hard to come by. There were tears and a short talk and the Lord's Prayer led by an old Amish bishop. One parent said it was a sacred moment and deeply sad. But there was peace, and the Lord's presence was so real.

At 10:45, the boys rang the bell. With so many boys pulling the rope, the bell stuck. The boys climbed up to the roof and rang the school bell manually. As the ringing of the bell sounded over Bart Township, love and healing and peace began to settle over the wounded community This was the start of a new normal.

On October 9, teacher Emma Zook resumed teaching, but in a nearby garage.

The press

At 10:45 on October 12, ten days after the shooting, demolition of the West Nickel Mines School began. In less than an hour, the schoolhouse was torn down and hauled away in dumpsters, escorted by police to an undisclosed landfill so no souvenir hunters could claim any artifacts.

Three and four days after the tragedy, five funerals were held: one for Roberts, three for three of the girls, and one for the two Miller sisters. Within an hour after the shooting and during the funerals, the media flocked to the little village of Nickel Mines, where 60 to 80 people live. Newspaper reporters and TV trucks and vans headquartered in nearby parking lots, and within what seemed liked minutes, the schoolhouse was broadcast worldwide. Local flags flew at half-mast.

The one-and-a-half-mile drive to the cemetery was so congested with news media and spectators that the state police provided dozens of troopers to guard the route and several helicopters to patrol the air space. Two troopers rode horses in front of the funeral processions to ensure no media would get out of hand, despite repeated requests not to photograph the funeral. It happened anyway. One woman even tried to dress Amish, hoping to attend the one funeral. She was quickly discovered because she wore a red dress. Amish women wear black at funerals.

Forgiveness and love

As the Lord's Prayer teaches us to ask forgiveness for our debts as we forgive our debtors, so began the Amish ritual of forgiving. First, one of the Amish bishops visited Mrs. Roberts and expressed forgiveness. Some 15 Amish families attended Roberts' funeral at a nearby church in Georgetown, one mile away.

Suddenly the media focused on forgiveness. Worldwide, the practice of forgiveness was explored and, to a degree, exploited. There were soon story writers visiting the families of the deceased, getting material for books. Although we didn't feel worthy of the publicity, we tried to stay humble as people wanted to talk about our "goodness."

There were many miracles as the five survivors were recuperating. One girl regained the use of her shattered shoulder. Another recovered the use of her hand, although she can't lift her arm very high. The most severely injured girl became more responsive. She began to smile and seemed to understand words, but she needs a feeding tube and cannot talk or walk. Mr. Roberts' mother went to this girl's home every day for an extended period to help with her therapy.

A miracle of love started to unfold almost from day one. Several local McDonald's restaurants brought food for the funerals. Soon money and mail came pouring in. The local fire station offered space for volunteers to handle the gifts of money, which was put toward paying medical expenses. Money came from all over the world. One school in Africa sent money, mostly in coins, for the Nickel Mines children.

We Amish have been humbled and blessed by the compassion and sincere love shown by outsiders during and after this terrible tragedy. There were remarkable responses and support from the first responders and the state and local police who assisted in road blocks and other basic needs of this sort. Nor can we forget the medical teams and counselors who offered their therapy and counseling services to the survivors after the shooting. Some continued this for years afterward. Many volunteers gave their time to processing the mail and donations, some continuing for years after the event.

About a month after the school building came down, there was talk of putting up a new schoolhouse. Soon land was available, and the township zoning officer and building inspector quickly got the paperwork and permits ready. In early December of 2006, ground was broken. By January 2007, the new school was under roof. Early in the spring, Teacher Emma and her pupils moved in. By then, some of those who were injured in the shooting were well enough to go back to school.

Although the Nickel Mines community was still struggling with terrifying memories, hope began to return. The new schoolhouse was named New Hope.

CHAPTER THIRTY

A Sabbath at Conestoga Retreat

At 6:30 in the morning on January 18, Katie and I headed out the drive with our trusty horse, Victor. We turned north on Leacock Road, then north on Hess Road, and continued north on Hershey Avenue. Now we were in Mennonite country—nice, level farmland—heading east on Conestoga Creek Road. We crossed the Conestoga Creek through a rustic covered bridge and arrived in the *Wava lant* (Weaverland). We went north again, now on Cidermill Road to Crooked Lane, the location of Conestoga Retreat. It's about a 13-mile trip, although it seemed a bit further since it was in the winter-time pre-dawn and on a cloudy morning.

This retreat facility was built as a support for the Old Order Amish and those Mennonites who belong to the Old Order Weaverland and Groffdale conferences, as well as the Stauffer Mennonites. It is a place for conservative Christian married couples to receive Christian counseling.

Offering care and support

The building has seven little apartments for couples to live in while they receive counseling. There is also a large, well equipped woodworking shop where the residents can work, making items to sell, or to create hobby items; one made a model of his homestead. Sometimes they get orders to make our Lancaster-style, folding-leg church benches.

Downstairs in the house is a large sewing room with Bernina, state-of-the-art sewing machines where the women sew items to sell. Several quilts were also in progress. There are plenty of projects to keep the men and the women busy. Two of the women were taking care of their small babies; one was eight weeks old.

This was the weekend that our district minister and his wife, Sam and Rachel Fisher, served as hosts, so they invited several church folks to come on Sunday. Our two ministers and three of us couples arrived at eight in the morning. The seven resident men were soon at the barn feeding our horses and visiting with us. I like our Amish custom of shaking hands and greeting everyone with a smile. We all visited with the residents and asked where they were from.

At 8:15, minister Sam came out to the barn and shook hands all around, and then we men headed to the Retreat Building. We all shook hands with the women and took our seats in the approximately 12' × 27' meeting room. It was a bit unusual to have our Amish worship service with a digital clock on the wall, carpeted floors, ceiling lights, and fans. We typically meet for worship in homes with removable partitions, large sheds, or barns.

At 8:30 the service started with an announcement that we would sing verses one and two of the 28-verse "Sermon on the Mount Hymn" written by Hans Benz. We followed that with the "Lobelied," led by four of the residents. A Mifflin County man led the first verse; verse two was led by a man from Kilgore, Ohio; verse three was led by another man from Kilgore; and the last verse a man from Coral, Michigan, led.

Preacher Sam Fisher gave the opening; then we all knelt for silent prayer. Matthew 5 was read by Preacher John Yoder. Preacher Johnny Fisher, Jr. had the sermon and read Matthew 6. Then Johnny asked for testimonies from the ministers and some of the lay men. We all knelt again, and Johnny read a prayer. We finished by singing verses three and four of the "Sermon on the Mount Hymn," and the service was over. Two little Yoder boys sat quietly during the service, listening and gazing about at the different atmosphere around them.

It was a mild, cloudy January day, and at noon it started to rain. We had been noticing six playful squirrels outside the window, frisking about, eating from the ear corn that was on a feeder at the one tree.

Good food and visiting

As soon as the benediction was made, the women scurried to the kitchen and set out the fellowship meal—snitz pies, sliced meat and cheese, bread, coffee, and tea. Mrs. Fisher had prepared the pie fixings at home before coming to the Retreat Center. The residents helped her bake the pies yesterday.

The residents had set up tables that morning so we were soon able to eat. After the meal, the visiting began. We talked about the residents' occupations at home, their families, and their style of *coppa* (prayer coverings). We sang for an hour out of the *Christian Hymnal* and then went back to visiting. It was soon time for us visitors to say our goodbyes and head south to our native Pequea with many precious memories of our newly made friends at Conestoga Retreat. Sam and Rachel Fisher stayed as hosts until Monday.

As we drove through Weaverland and Groffdale and on to our Pequea home turf, we reflected on what has been accomplished in the last 15 years in a plainfolk setting to help our members who are mentally stressed. In Pennsylvania alone, Philhaven Hospital created Green Pasture Clinic for the Plain Communities. Whispering Hope was established in Franklin County, and both Sunrise Meadows and Conestoga Retreat were developed in Lancaster County, along with Kurtz Homestead for single women. We give thanks to the Lord for this blessing and continue in prayer for those seeking help to have their emotional and mental health restored.

CHAPTER THIRTY-ONE

Life in God's Hands

My wife Katie and I had a miraculous incident in the summer of 2009. It was a beautiful summer Sunday in June. We had been visiting with my sister's family about six miles from our home, when we got word that our nephew's little five-year-old had fallen off their spring wagon and been killed. We spent several hours at their home offering our condolences. So it got quite late as we drove home in our horse and carriage.

It was about 10:30 on that dark, moonless night as we headed west on Harvest Drive, about ¾ of a mile from our home in Gordonville. As we came up to Leacock Road, I looked south and then north and didn't see anything close. I saw headlights in the south, about ⅓ mile away coming out of Gordonville. There is a little hill on Leacock Road, so I couldn't see what kind of vehicle it was, nor how fast it was traveling. I was sure I could easily pull out before the headlights got to us.

We had a new horse, and as I pulled out, he was a bit slow to get going. Just as I got out onto Leacock Road, the vehicle shot over the hill at a terrible speed and was instantly on us. Now I saw that it was a single headlight, a motorcycle coming right at us. It was impossible to get out of its way. There was a screech and a crash as the cycle hit our horse.

Oh, my, I had a terrifying thought. I had pulled out in front of the cycle. I stopped the horse; surprisingly, he was still on his feet, although I feared he had a broken leg. To my right, about 15 feet away, lay the cycle rider, flat out on the road. The cycle was on its side about 30 feet further along Leacock Road. Oh, dear, more horrible thoughts. I killed a man. There will be a hearing, and I will go to jail.

If only...

I gave the reins to my wife and got out of the carriage. Oh, how will we get help? As an answer to prayer, a buggy was coming west on Harvest Drive with two young boys inside. "Do you have a cell phone?" I yelled. "Yes," they answered, and immediately called 911, reporting an accident at the Leacock Road and Harvest Drive intersection. Thankfully, the Gordonville Fire Station is just about ⅓ mile away, and its siren sounded about 90 seconds later. The Gordonville ambulance also responded almost instantly and came roaring to the scene.

As I walked over to the cycle driver, I was certain he was deader than a doornail. Suddenly I heard a loud moan, then louder moans, and with great effort he sat up. "Sit still," I said, "you might be hurt."

"I'm fine," he said, struggling to his feet. "I want to get going. I gotta get out of here." He walked over to his cycle and tried to set it upright with me helping him a bit. He couldn't find the kickstand so he could support the cycle, which I eventually found. Just then the ambulance arrived, and Kate, one of Gordonville's best first-responder personnel, was in charge.

The fire truck came and the firemen set up a roadblock. Soon a policeman was there. He helped check out the cycle driver, who, by now, the ambulance crew had loaded into the ambulance. He had a bad cut on his chin. Kate was cleaning out the cut when I reached in to give him his bandana, which had caught on my carriage mirror. Kate said, "Listen, Sam, you just cool it. Don't come in the ambulance. We'll take care of everything."

The policeman got my name and address, and then got the cycle driver's information. He was from Bowmansville and had been at a party in Paradise. The cop told me the cycle driver had been drinking and was going way too fast. He made him walk a straight line and looked into his eyes. It was quite obvious he was inebriated. The ambulance took the cycle driver to the hospital. Soon his wife and friends came and hauled the cycle away, which had only a broken mirror and taillight.

Meanwhile, Katie drove our team to the nearby schoolyard. A fireman examined our horse; miraculously there was only a cut on his one back leg and scrapes on his belly. The policeman explained that no charges would be filed against me. So we finally drove home, now quite late at night. Sometime later the vet came and checked out the horse and left only a salve for the cut.

Our carriage had only a slight scrape on its shafts. How did the cyclist slide under our horse with so little damage? Surely God's hand was over us and him. Although it all happened too fast to really know, it seems the cycle driver skidded about 70 feet, then hit the horse, which knocked him off his bike. He then slid under the horse, flat out and stopped just past the horse. He had no broken bones; only a bad cut. His bandana, which had been wrapped around his long hair, flew off and landed on our left headlight, still tied as a headband.

We got to bed about 1:00 a.m. with thankful hearts to God for his protecting hand.

Elmer's evening

Our son Elmer was also under God's care that Sunday night. As he was hitching up to go home after a singing, something startled his horse, and he bolted and knocked Elmer over. Elmer got up right away, a bit dazed, but was able to finish hitching up and drive the 10 miles home.

Next morning at the breakfast table he said, "*Dat*, my jaw doesn't feel right." So we made a trip to the doctor, who said his jaw was cracked. Then we made a visit to the local orthodontist, who said his jaw was broken. So the orthodontist fastened his lower jaw to his top one with rubber bands and clips, and Elmer was on a drinkable diet for eight weeks. He would put anything he wanted to eat—salads, veggies, potatoes, fruit—in an air-motor-powered blender, mix in milk so it went through a straw, and then slurp it up. After the bands came off, his jaws were back to normal. Amazingly, he didn't even lose much weight. Again we felt God's protecting hand.

CHAPTER THIRTY-TWO

A Week Without My Gordonville Peach

Let me tell you how our one son Elmer and I survived an almost Class 5 Emergency when my wife and another son, Isaac, went to Trigg County, Kentucky, 900 miles from home, to visit our children Ammon and Mary Stoltzfoos.

The near-crisis began on September 20, 2010, when I took Peach and our son Isaac to Bird-in-Hand Farm Supply, a 2½-mile jaunt.

At 4:20 in the morning, the Kentucky travel bus came cruising west on Route 340 and swung into the parking lot. All sorts of souls were waiting to board the bus. A big load of potatoes and lots of boxes were loaded into the luggage compartment. My wife and son took their seats. With a wave and a roar, they were off!

No good to wish her back now. The house was very empty. Well, Monday night supper was easy. Daughter-in-law Sadie Joy invited us to come for a delicious meal. Great—we had no dishes to wash. Son Elmer packed his lunch for the next day. And we knew *Mam* had made two pans of cornmeal mush for breakfast, as well as instructions about how to make oatmeal and fry the mush. Getting breakfast ready would be a piece of cake in the morning. So she said, or so I thought.

Breakfast time came all too soon. The mush turned out okay, but the oatmeal boiled over and the eggs were almost rock hard. The toast was fine. Elmer ate his breakfast quickly and was out the lane at ten of six to meet his ride. So I ate my breakfast alone. It took me some time to figure out how to get the drip pan out of the oven, so I didn't have time to do the dishes. I just put them in to soak, which was easy enough.

A sick horse

I had a real crisis though that morning when Elmer's horse, Violet, was flat. Oh, my. So I called the vet again. She had been sick on Saturday, but it just seemed like colic. Now it was serious. The vet had been there Monday and said he suspected West Nile Virus. Oh dear, this horse was Elmer's pride and joy.

I had a meeting that morning at the Mennonite Library, so I left early. I fully expected the horse would be crow feed when I returned at noon. But miracles do happen. Our farmer son Gideon reported that Violet got up alone, but oh, what a sight. She didn't eat or drink. She just hung her head. She could barely walk, but she ate a little grass in the meadow. The vet came late in the afternoon and gave her $150.00 worth of attention. Poor checkbook.

Tuesday evening our daughter Linda gave us supper. What a relief, although we did the dishes. We were worrying about Violet. The DMSO medication that the vet gave left a bad smell all over this part of planet Earth.

Wednesday morning I jumped awake at 4:45 and checked on Violet. She just gave me a sad look that said, I'm sick, can't you see? She ate like a woman on a strict diet and drank only a bit of water.

Managing the kitchen

Breakfast-making went better because I had learned how to streamline meal-making. I put the folding table next to where we ate, right beside the fridge door, so if we forgot anything, it was just an arm's length away. Elmer would leave just a bit before seven. I and our grandson Sam David left at 6:15 with a driver to pick up some items at West Chester. We soaked the dishes again. My wife would have had a fit. The sink looked a fright.

Dinner-time at noon was more routine. I ate a sandwich, cereal, yogurt, and peanut butter crackers. And I washed the dishes. Yuck! It took lots of scrubbing with steel wool, even though I had soaked the dishes.

I had to get back to work. Sweeping the floor would have to wait. Our daughter Linda made supper. Good! No washing dishes that evening.

Elmer went off to his youth-group practice singing. The house seemed dark and lonely at bedtime.

Thursday morning breakfast went well. The mush was good. We got the eggs and toast just right. Elmer once again was off to work a little before seven. I put the dishes in to soak.

It was another morning when I was too busy to sweep. I wanted to get our new basement cabinets painted as a surprise for my wife. That took most of the day. I also helped a neighbor get ready to pour concrete.

That evening our supper and bedtime were late. Fortunately I had done the dishes at noon. You know, they don't take long if you do them right away! I just stacked everything in the dishrack as I washed them. A busy schoolteacher once said that air-dried dishes don't get germs from wiping. I found that to be good practical logic at a time like this.

An overnight guest?!

Friday morning came quickly. Breakfast went very well. Grandson Michael and I left at 5:45 a.m. to pour four yards of concrete in our neighbor's barn. I also took our horse to the blacksmith. Dinner was routine, but then another crisis came. Preacher John Glick stopped in and asked, "Do you want out-of-state company?"

Oh, dear, my, wife's not home. The house looks a fright. . . "Well sure, who are they?" I asked.

"Sam J. Swartzentruber of Huvelton, New York. He wants to be near Gordonville so he can walk to the sale tomorrow."

"Oh, well, let him come." I troweled some more concrete and then headed home. Thankfully son Elmer came home on time and swept the kitchen. My, there was so much dirt. Then Elmer put the rest of the kitchen in order. And at 6:00 p.m., visitor Sam came, a tall lanky man with a coal-black beard and a big smile.

Daughter Linda came to our rescue and made a delicious supper. Sam was quite a talker, and we had lots to discuss. Bedtime was a bit late.

The next morning, son Elmer made pancakes and eggs. Sam J. ate heartily and had many stories. He said that when he was ordained minister in 1996, he told his wife, "Now we will no longer laugh or travel." But these many years later, Sam burst out laughing, "Isn't coming 700 miles to the little village of Gordonville traveling?" he admitted.

Well, Sam made his goodbye and thanked us for the bed and breakfast, stuffed his pockets full of candy, and set out for the sale. Now I had to get the house in order. Peach was coming home at 9:30 this morning. Hurray!

Cleaning up

I slipped out of doing the dishes because it was Elmer's turn. I decided to mop the kitchen floor and filled a bucket with hot water. But what does Katie add? I found more than a half dozen containers of cleaners, and which cloth is the right one for floor cleaning? My, it's going to take a college degree to make the correct choice. Maybe we should call a congressional hearing to decide.

I finally consult daughter Linda, and thankfully she informs me. So I mop the floor, getting all the areas, including under the table and the recliner. I shake out the rugs, mop the bathroom, and clean the tub and vanity. The place looks presentable. It passes our daughter's critical eye. At 9:00 I hitch up, and the grandson and I hurry off to meet Katie at Bird-in-Hand Farm Supply.

Oh, dear, she is nowhere to be seen. The bus had been there, unloaded the Lancaster folks, and left. There's a big benefit sale and flea market across Route 340, and hundreds of folks are there. It took some looking, but I finally found my peach, and home we went. Once again the meals were made, the floors were swept, and our home had a proper homemaker. I had learned firsthand that housekeeping operations aren't easy, nor do they run by perpetual motion. And it was very good to have her presence in the place. I was very thankful.

Author Sam Stoltzfus is a regular columnist for The Connection, a monthly magazine published in Indiana, whose purpose is "Connecting Our Amish Communities."

CHAPTER THIRTY-THREE

A *Connection* Wedding

At 3:30 in the morning, headlights shone in our driveway. It was May 8, and a driver had come to take us to Mark Yoder and Doretta Fry's wedding in Indiana. We headed up Route 501 to pick up Jake R. Stoltzfus in Meyerstown. Our next stop was in Nittany Valley at Levi Eshes. Levi is a *Connection* writer, and his wife, Sylvia, had a big breakfast ready at 6:30. After breakfast, they joined us on the trip as we continued west on Route 80 to the Ohio Turnpike and then on to the Indiana Turnpike.

It felt like a short trip, even though we were four couples who barely knew each other, but we each had a lot to say. Levi had been up half the night making hay and had had only two hours of sleep, so he caught up a bit on his Zzzzs. By 3:30 in the afternoon, we arrived at the home of our friend Floyd Miller. We hitched up Floyd's rig and cruised three miles south for a quick visit with

Dan A. and Katie Hostetler. I first met Dan in 1965 when we both were volunteers during the Palm Sunday tornado reconstruction. We had a fast tour of his library and then drove back to Floyds for a delicious supper and a good night's rest.

We woke to a beautiful Hoosier State sunrise, ready to enjoy the wedding. Thanks to Doretta's precise map, we easily found her home, the Ervin Fry residence. After meeting and shaking hands with other wedding guests for over an hour, we were ushered into the house. At 9:00 the services began with singing page 508 in the *Ausbund*. (We Easterners always begin by singing page 378.) Then the two best men each led two verses of the next hymn, the "Lobelied," following which we sang page 139, verse 4.

Preacher Harvey Lambright gave the opening sermon about the creation story and included good advice for Mark and Doretta. He cautioned against a husband and wife being too silent, an opposite form of communication. Cletus Wingard read the customary wedding scripture, which is part of Matthew 19. It was the first wedding for Bishop Jones, but he had a well thought-out sermon. It was just like a Lancaster wedding sermon, including the Tobias story from the *Apochrypha*.

Bishop Jones often switched to English, a kind deed for the many English folks present. He married Mark and Doretta at 11:30. Then he read the marriage vows in English, as well as a fitting poem in English. Bishop Jones also told of a college professor whose elderly wife was ailing. He didn't want her to go to a nursing home, choosing instead to care for her at home. He said it's good to stay together as a couple till death parts us. Jones also quoted from Proverbs 31, about a virtuous woman. The last hymn we sang was page 712, the same as we use in Lancaster to close a wedding service.

After the wedding, Mark and Doretta drove to the reception site in a small four-wheel wagon pulled by two Haflinger ponies. "Just married" was written on the back of the wagon, and several balloons fluttered along. They made a charming picture heading west on Topeka's Main Street.

An at-home reception meal for 400

The Yoders spared no effort to serve their wedding guests. A huge plastic roof covered the space between their barn and carriage shed. This provided an approximately 80′ × 100′ area to set up seven long tables. Two more long tables were set up in part of the barn, so that about 400 guests could eat at one time. The ushers took good care of us Pennsylvania folks. We ate at one of the first tables. In Lancaster we have our customary *Eck* table (positioned in the corner of the room) for the wedding party. In Indiana, Mark and Doretta and the *nava* sitters (their best boy and girl) sat at a separate table.

The food was delicious, and there was plenty. Almost everything was passed around twice. The mixed fruit was plentiful and was on the tables when we sat down so we could have some as an appetizer. It was there again at supper.

I was amazed at how efficiently the cooking crew was organized. Each table had a team of waiters. After those who were seated first had finished eating, dishpans were hustled in, with the same waiters doing the dishes and resetting the tables for the next round of guests. The tables had been set first by family and friends four days before the wedding. Then about 20 minutes before Jones married Mark and Doretta, the table waiters came into the wedding service so they could be there for at least part of the service. But soon after the marriage vows, the table waiters marched out again.

I didn't see any hostlers helping unhitch the teams like we have in Lancaster.

Logistical ideas from the Indiana Amish!

One thing we could borrow from the Indiana folks is to have the kitchen staff eat dinner first, at 10:00. In Pennsylvania, they don't eat until everyone else is finished.

I wondered how each person knew what to do and when. Clearly, Mary Alice, Mark's mother, had it all precisely organized on her computer. One woman told me to go in the cook's room and look on the south wall. There a big schematic had been printed out and hung up, the heartbeat of an Indiana Amish wedding. In the Lancaster community, we have a woman with a paper directing who does what and when. Another thing we could use in Lancaster is their cooking trailer, a 36-foot camper with six stoves, a 6' × 6' cooler room, sinks, and a hot water heater. The whole thing looks very practical. I wonder what it costs.

After the dinner, the groom's mother, Mary Alice Yoder, and Nancy Amor, editors of *The Connection*, hosted an important meeting for all the *Connection* writers attending the wedding. We gathered in the back lawn away from the wedding hustle and bustle. I enjoyed meeting the other columnists and hearing how each one got started and how they were encouraged to write. Many began writing at the urging of the editors, just to help get the magazine started.

As the group introduced themselves, I was impressed by how many good writers there are. I don't count myself among them. Everyone's story was different. Some started with their wives' encouragement; some write best at the last minute; some work in human services and do well detailing that; and some just write! The writers are a good cross-section of small-town and small-farm Amish.

Yes, this business meeting could have been in a fancy building with comfy chairs in a plush conference room, but it was much better under a bright Indiana sun with Nancy as chairwoman. One question was answered: Doretta, the newlywed, would continue on the staff. Mary Alice also said there would be a June issue, which had to be put together in the middle of all the wedding preparations and all the sewing! (By the way what was that pretty wedding dress color? Answer: Sage Green.)

Indiana hospitality

Later we sat in the garage with the family, singing out of the *Ausbund* while Mark and Doretta opened their wedding gifts. We observed many guests leaving while others were coming. We also discovered that the Pennsylvania folks had been invited for the daytime services but not for supper. But Mary Alice kindly extended our invitation into the evening. Thank you to the Yoders for having us!

The evening meal was served first at 4:30 for friends and church families who had just come. The cooks and table waiters and more new folks were served at 6:00, and then at 7:00, the youth and Mark's and Doretta's families ate.

After the meal, many of the youth came to Mark and Doretta to shake their hands and wish them well. And then most of them sat down to sing wedding songs that had been printed on paper and laid out over the evening tables.

At 8:30 we said our good-byes and headed east to Home Sweet Home. Thanks again, folks, for your kind hospitality. The day was a memory-maker. And we enjoyed observing how the Indiana folks handle large weddings. Over 1500 meals were served at this one.

We also learned how Mark and Doretta began dating. They had been with a youth group who often went singing for old folks and shut-ins. They became acquainted, began dating, and decided to marry. Young folks starting their homes is the foundation of our Amish culture.

We drove home with many reflections, among them that our wedding heritage is just as strong in Indiana as it is in Pennsylvania. It is something we all need to cherish. Let's be thankful for our young people and for the grace of God which blesses our marriages.

For more information about this book and other titles published by Walnut Street Books, please visit www.walnutstreetbooks.com.

About the Author

Sam S. Stoltzfus lives on a farm with his wife, Katie, just outside the village of Gordonville in eastern Lancaster County, Pennsylvania. A member of the Old Order Amish, he is now retired from farming and is active in the Pequea Bruderschaft Library and the Lancaster Mennonite Historical Society.

He is retired from building gazebos and sheds, and with Katie processes and sells horseradish.

A train buff since childhood, because of the many daily trains that crossed through the neighborhood, Sam also enjoys writing regular columns for *The Connection*, a monthly magazine with a large Amish readership.

Sam and Katie are the parents of nine children, 51 grandchildren, and three great-grandchildren.